Handbook to Higher Consciousness: The Workbook

Ken Keyes, Jr. and Penny Keyes

A daily practice book
to help you increase
your heart-to-heart loving
and happiness

D0873045

Love Line Books
700 Commercial Avenue
Coos Bay, OR 97420

About This Book

Your purchase of any Love Line book helps to build a more loving and caring world. The authors receive no royalties. All surplus goes to a nonprofit organization dedicated to teaching Living Love and the Science of Happiness.

Handbook to Higher Consciousness: The Workbook may be obtained through your local bookstore, or you may order it from the Ken Keyes College Bookroom, 790 Commercial Avenue, Coos Bay, OR 97420 for $5.95 plus $1.50 for postage and handling.

Up to five pages of this book may be freely quoted or reprinted without permission, provided credit is given in the following form:

© 1989 Love Line Books
ISBN: 0-915972-16-6   (alkaline paper)

First Printing: March 1989   25,000 copies

Thanks!

First we wish to acknowledge the countless people who over nearly two decades have used the Living Love Methods in their lives. Their living experience has enabled us to distill the system to make it increasingly effective.

Dave Carrothers and Elizabeth Moore of Love Line Books originally proposed and constantly encouraged us to produce this workbook. Ann Hauser of Love Line Books added her spirit and talent to every phase of production: typesetting, editing, and drawing the delightful cartoons on the work pages. Claudia Lowman creatively designed the drawings on the chapter title pages.

Anne Kelley, Tully Strong, and David White gave us valuable feedback based on their use of these daily worksheets. Aura Wright, one of our outstanding trainers, has contributed many excellent suggestions based on her extensive experience in leading Living Love workshops.

To these and others we give our heartfelt appreciation.

Ken Keyes, Jr. and Penny Keyes

Contents

For Easy Reference

Benefits
of
This
Workbook

This workbook can help you increase the happiness and effectiveness in your life. It will show you how to take the principles presented in *Handbook to Higher Consciousness* by Ken Keyes, Jr. and apply them in a practical way to enhance your daily living. It supports you in taking time each day to focus on your inner growth—and thus gain experience and skill using the Living Love Methods.

We have found that daily practice is needed to become proficient in using these methods "on the spot" when you have a problem in your life. Just knowing the methods intellectually doesn't automatically make them effective in skillfully meeting life's challenges. However, it's your first step. Using them regularly is the *only* way to integrate them into your personal experience.

As with any new skill, learning these methods takes time and effort. With experience, you will gain the ability to apply them in any situation. By reviewing your day with this workbook, you can remind yourself of the *living love* you can create in each moment. And you will become increasingly aware of your demanding programming that is blocking your experience of that love.

By giving yourself the gift of daily practice, you can enjoy these ten benefits:

Actively supporting yourself in making your personal growth a high priority in your life.

Giving yourself a daily reminder that your programming—*not your life situations*—is determining your internal experience.

Learning to recognize your greatest opportunities for consciousness growth.

Developing skill with the methods presented in the *Handbook.*

Improving your emotional flexibility in responding to various situations.

Whittling away addictive demands that keep you trapped in the illusion of separateness.

Reducing upsetting emotions, and eventually changing self-destructive patterns.

Strengthening your ability to love and accept yourself and others.

Finding more inner peace and a deeper happiness and joy.

Increasingly bringing the power of love into your life.

Fifteen Minutes Each Day

When we say "15 minutes a day to higher consciousness," we are expressing our confidence that if you regularly give at least 15 minutes a day to focusing your mind on your consciousness growth, you will notice changes in your attitude toward yourself and others—and in your reactions to the inevitable life situations that you wish were different. We regard using these daily worksheeets for three months as the minimal time needed to make significant desired changes in your mental habits.

While there is no limit to how intensely one may dedicate oneself to personal growth, we do caution against setting yourself up with great expectations—just to abandon doing any work altogether because you find the pace or time too impractical. So often one enthusiastically embarks on a self-improvement program, only to have the interest fizzle away until the aspirations—and the program—are virtually forgotten.

We suggest that you support yourself by setting aside a specific time in your day. At the beginning you may want to allow a half hour until you familiarize yourself with the methods. Choose a time that you will find easiest to devote to these practice sheets whether in the morning, mid-day, or evening. However, the workbook is oriented toward reflecting on your day in the evening, and clearing out internal conflicts before going to sleep.

Make a commitment to yourself to stay with it for three months so that habits can be established. After this time, you can assess whether you've noticed a difference in your day-to-day experience of life. If you have, you'll probably want to keep going. If you haven't, then perhaps this practice is not for you. There are lots of wonderful growth systems available to us. The important thing is to find something that works for you, and to stick with it so you have direction when the going gets tough.

Our experience has been that when we work (or play) with these methods on a daily basis, we are reminding ourselves of more effective choices in handling our attitudes, interactions, and situations. By using these worksheets each day, we can keep alive throughout the day a spark of remembrance of what we humans can create in our precious lives. As you fill these pages, you may find yourself more aware of your automatic unpleasant reactions. You'll discover alternative approaches you can use in sticky situations. You can discover what you truly value most—and how you've been sabotaging yourself in achieving it.

We think consciousness growth is an exciting and fascinating part of life, and that, in the end, it makes the most difference in our overall personal experience of life. Regardless of the dramas we play out, the internal emotional experience created moment to moment by the programming in our minds is what will matter most.

Fifteen minutes a day is not much to invest in exchange for increased satisfaction, effectiveness, peace, love, and happiness. This daily practice book will simply aid you in *using* for your growth what your life brings you each day. To the extent that you listen to your thoughts, consciously feel your emotions and body sensations, and apply the power of your imagination, you will be *doing* the practice—not just learning about it or knowing about it. *Doing* it is what will give you the growth and happiness you want.

7

A Quick Review of the Basics

$$\mathbf{T}$$his workbook is designed to enrich the lives of over one million people who have read *Handbook to Higher Consciousness* since it was published in 1972. In case it's been some time since you read the *Handbook*, here is a brief review of the basics you need to do the daily exercises. As you use this workbook, you can deepen your insights if you gradually and absorbingly study the *Handbook*.

Preferences vs. Demands

You can enormously increase your happiness by changing the automatic mental habits that make you 1) react negatively, critically, fearfully, or judgmentally to things you do not want in your life, or 2) chase after or cling to things you addictively do want. Suppose your supervisor tells you that you must work three hours extra tonight, and you had plans for the evening. How do you feel? Most people emotionally react to this by making themselves upset with anger, irritation, frustration, and resentment. They feel separate from whomever or whatever they believe is the cause of this undesired change. Their automatic mental habits destroy their enjoyment of the evening. Notice the difference between demanding and preferential programming:

HOW OUR MINDS WORK

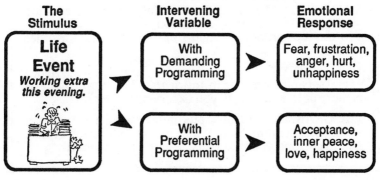

The Stimulus	Intervening Variable	Emotional Response
Life Event *Working extra this evening.*	With Demanding Programming	Fear, frustration, anger, hurt, unhappiness
	With Preferential Programming	Acceptance, inner peace, love, happiness

You can use Living Love to help you enjoy your life even when things don't go the way you want them to. To do this, you must understand that the outside happening (being told you have to work three hours extra tonight) combines with your internal demanding programming (inside you're demanding that your boss not say you must work extra tonight), which makes you automatically trigger anger, dismay, frustration, resentment, etc.

The Living Love Methods are tools which help you creatively cope with the many things that happen in your life that you don't like. These techniques let you turn lemons into lemonades. They enable you to become more emotionally accepting and effective in responding to undesired life situations in a way that harmoniously cooperates with others and maintains your personal enjoyment.

How does it work in the above example? You begin by recognizing that you have what we call an *addictive demand* in your mind which somehow got put in there earlier in your life (see definitions below). That demanding programming is the *immediate, practical cause* of your being upset. This insight helps you go beyond the illusion that unexpectedly working three hours extra in the evening was the sole *cause* of your anger, frustration, or resentment.

ADDICTIVE DEMAND: An expectation or model that makes you feel upset or unhappy if it is not satisfied. A demand that causes body tension, separating emotions, and/or mind disturbance.

PREFERENCE: A desire that does not trigger any separating feelings or tensions in your mind or body *whether or not* your desire is satisfied.

SEPARATING EMOTION: A feeling stemming from the separate-self such as fear, frustration, or anger that creates in you the illusion of alienation from yourself and/or other people.

UNHAPPINESS: The conscious or unconscious experience of any separating feeling in any degree. When unhappiness is more or less continual, you experience suffering.

PROGRAMMING: Conscious or unconscious instructions set in your mind that play a part in interpreting life events, and in creating your thoughts, feelings, and actions.

The Secrets of Happiness

Your addictive demands trigger separating emotions that create your unhappiness. That which you emotionally demand to avoid can be just as much an addictive demand as something you emotionally demand to have. The first step in dealing effectively with an addictive demand is to be aware that you have an addiction. You know you have an addiction if you notice any of the following:

> You feel tension or tightness in your body.
> You experience separating emotions. (See inside back cover.)
> You keep telling yourself over and over that things "should" be different.
> Your life seems bogged down by a "problem."

Changing your demands to preferences can enormously increase your happiness. You provide yourself with a much more enjoyable experience when you *prefer* that your evening not be tied up—but you no longer *demand* it. When you prefer that things be different from the way they are, you can enjoy your life even though:

1) You can still want what you want.
2) You can still try to make changes.
3) You can still think you're "right."

With a preference, you just don't have to feel upset or unhappy! Your friends and family will find you more pleasant to be around at such times. You thus *transform your experience of life* in a situation that you previously thought was forcing you to feel upset.

Some people hold on to their fear or righteous anger; they think they need it to act appropriately to things they don't like. But fear over not enough security, frustration about not enough sensations, or anger about being unable to control things is not a part of "the good life." Exchanging demands for preferences is a solution that often works like magic.

When we talk about accepting a situation or behavior that you don't like (in yourself or another person), we are referring to your *internal emotional acceptance.* This here-and-now emotional acceptance does not keep you from trying to

11

change the situation or behavior—or prevent it in the future. However you decide to respond outwardly, that decision will be made with greater clarity if you operate from a preference (internal emotional acceptance) than from an addictive demand (emotional resistance, clinging, or ignoring).

Upleveling demands to preferences is a skill you can acquire. With practice, you will no longer be buffeted around by all kinds of things that happen in your life that you previously thought made you unhappy. You will become the *master of your experience*. You will develop a new energy of enjoyment, fun, and ability to handle "adversity." You will profoundly experience the joy of living—regardless of what is happening around you. And you will become more effective in focusing your energy and making changes in things that are changeable—instead of beating your head against the brick walls of life that are not changeable now.

Practice in this new mental skill will set the stage for increasing your self-appreciation and self-esteem—even when you do and say things that you wish you hadn't. It will also encourage you to appreciate and love other people *unconditionally*; you may not like what they do or say, but you will learn to perceive them as a beautiful *essence of humanity* behind their particular programming which creates their actions and words in each moment of their lives.

This cause-and-effect concept (your programming determines your inner experience) is easy to explain and understand—and sometimes our ingrained mental habits make it difficult to apply in heated situations. Our success in developing the skill of upleveling our demands into preferences is a vital factor in determining whether we will live the happiest life possible. By using this workbook, you can move toward achieving a dynamic mental ability that will transform your life and allow you to discover a deeper joy of living.

Using Your Experiences

If you don't like the music that is coming out of your cassette player, you don't usually criticize the machine. You simply take out the program that was playing and replace it with a program you enjoy more. The Living Love Methods enable you to "reprogram" your wonderful mind. (We like to think of the mind as a "biocomputer" because it helps us be aware of both the working of the computer—and the program we put into it.)

Of course, it can be a lot easier to change a program in your cassette player that you don't like than to change a program in your mind. *However, if you want to feel happier, it is essential that you become an expert in changing the programs in your mind that make you feel separate from yourself or other people—and thus destroy your ability to love.*

The things you don't like in your life can be perceived as "gifts"—real opportunities to acquire the skill of transforming your experience into new dimensions of enjoyment, appreciation, and love for yourself and others!

At the beginning of the two worksheets for each day, you will write about "gifts" that your life has given you during the day: situations that triggered demands which made you upset. It is vital that you use your experience of each day to develop insight and perspective by pinpointing your demands. This use of your daily demands will fuel your growth.

Pinpointing Addictive Demands

In order to change any unwanted demanding habits of mind, it is helpful to first identify the demanding programming that is making you upset. Since your ego may resist this new way of dealing with your emotional turmoil, we urge you to say to yourself *every time you're upset*:

I create the experience of _____
                                (separating emotions)

because my programming demands that _____

_____
          (formulate precisely what you want)

It is easier to pinpoint your addictive demand when you identify which specific separating emotion(s) you are feeling. General terms such as "unhappy," "tense," or "insecure" keep you from honestly focusing on what is happening inside you. "Depressed" usually indicates multiple and/or conflicting addictive demands. Turn now to the list of separating emotions on the inside back cover of this workbook. Familiarize yourself with this emotional spectrum our minds can produce. You can use the list to help you label what you're feeling when you have an addictive demand.

Be Specific

Preferences are nondemanding desires or models you have of how you want things to be. When you operate with preferential programming, you can take outward action while feeling inwardly peaceful—no matter what happens. The purpose of pinpointing an addictive demand is to help you uplevel—change—it to a preference. A *specific* addictive demand is easier to uplevel than a *general* demand. By specific, we mean knowing *who* the demand is on (i.e., who you feel separate from), exactly *what* you're demanding, *when* you're wanting the demand met (covering only one point in time), and *where* you want the demand met.

We call the who, what, when, and where the "4 W's." It is important to be aware of the 4 W's of each of your demands. Your mind will be more inclined to uplevel a demand to a preference if it is specific. For example, there is no way your ego would be willing to let go of a *general* demand that "Mr. Jones treat me fairly." Your mind may, however, be willing to uplevel to a preference a *specific* demand that "Mr. Jones not ask me to work three hours extra tonight."

Pinpointing with an awareness of *who, what, when,* and *where* can take time and energy. *But if you don't keep working with your demands to get them specific, you'll be less successful in upleveling them to preferences.*

The easiest way to pinpoint your specific addictive demand is to focus on the exact moment when you felt the separating emotion(s). Recall your emotions as if that moment (or scene) were happening right now. Your demand can be about anything, including something that hasn't even happened. Use any of the following questions to help you pinpoint your demand.

In that situation:

What do you want? not want?

How do you feel he/she/you/it should be? Or shouldn't be?

What do you want him/her/you/it to do? Or not do?

How do you want him/her/you/it to be? Or not be?

If a magic genie appeared at that moment, what one thing would you ask for?

As you pinpoint your demand, you can make it more specific by:

Naming names ("Mr. Jones" instead of "somebody" or "my boss").

Spelling out exactly how you want the person, situation, object, *or you* to change ("Susan invite me to her party" is more specific than "Susan like me").

Focusing on the time you wanted something different ("Jim call me this afternoon" is more specific than "Jim call me").

An addictive demand can be silly, petty, impossible, or illogical. Remember: You can addictively demand *anything*. For pinpointing to be most useful, make it *specific*. Your ego may think your demand is specific enough, and it will often resist making it more specific. It knows being specific means you may be more willing to let it go, and your separate-self ego thinks its job is to make sure you hold on to each demand.

If you work with one scene at a time, you will find it easier to be specific. Focusing on specific addictions can bring perspective and insight. Often you may have more than one demand triggered in a given situation. If you do, use the form on page 13 to list each demand separately.

Unconditional Love

This workbook will help you bring the power of love into your life.

15

Many people can read the above sentence with some skepticism. They don't know what we mean by the "power of love." Does it mean that someone loves you so much that you have power over him or her? Does the "power of love" break your heart when a loved one dies or a relationship ends? Sounds like pretty dangerous stuff!

Most dictionaries generally define love as:

1) A feeling of warm personal attachment or deep affection, as for a parent, child, or friend.
2) Sexual passion or desire, or its gratification.

Great sages throughout history have pointed out that real love has no strings attached. It is a heartfelt, unconditional love that does not whirl like a weathercock with the daily happenings in one's life. *You love a person because he or she is there;* you do not require him or her to earn or "deserve" your love. For us, "Living Love" and "the power of love" refer to an *unconditional love in your heart.*

"Unconditional" means that your love is constant even if you don't like what a person is saying or doing. For example, a mother may not like the way her young baby spills its milk or keeps reaching for things it shouldn't touch. But the mother's love is usually not diminished by this unwanted behavior. This love is unconditional.

Your love must be unconditional to *experience its enormous power* for making your life work better. Threatening to withdraw love to control or intimidate people (e.g., "If you do that, I won't love you anymore") drains you of the love inside you; ultimately, you lose.

A basic principle in Living Love is "Love everyone unconditionally—including yourself." If you don't clearly understand what we mean by "unconditional love," you will regard this as impractical. How can you love a child molester or a murderer? How can you love your mate if he or she breaks agreements, squanders money, or does other things that you greatly dislike?

It is at this point that people become confused in their attempts to "live love." They mistakenly think that loving another person unconditionally means that they have to like everything the person does or says. This unfortunate lack of understanding destroys their ability to love steadily.

To increase your skill in loving unconditionally, it is essential to realize that you can totally dislike what people do or say, you can try to change them, and you can even throw them out of your home if they continue with this behavior. *You just don't throw them out of your heart!*

Loving unconditionally is sometimes a difficult skill for people to learn. But you must master it if you really want to bring its great benefits into your life. Through your successes and failures in life situations, you can gradually develop more and more skill in loving unconditionally.

To summarize briefly, the main goal to aim for as you use this daily practice book, is to increase your ability to

LOVE EVERYONE UNCONDITIONALLY— INCLUDING YOURSELF.

The biggest thing that keeps you from opening your heart with love in any moment is your demanding programming. An effective way to increase your happiness is to work directly with your addictive demands *as they arise*. Separating emotions, bodily tensions, and a churning mind are all sure signs of an addiction. Once you are in touch with your addictive programming, you can work on it using the methods laid out in the pages of this workbook.

It is essential to let yourself experience your separating feelings in order for you to use the Living Love Methods. You can honor and love yourself when you become aware of an addictive demand. Your demand is simply a programming that is keeping you from enjoying your life in any moment. You can regard it as a gift—an opportunity for you to learn to love more, and to increase the insight, effectiveness, and happiness in your life.

The next section will review four Living Love Methods that can help you uplevel your addictive demands into preferences.

The Four Methods

THE TWELVE PATHWAYS

CONSCIOUSNESS FOCUSING

LINKING THE SUFFERING WITH THE DEMAND

CENTERS OF CONSCIOUSNESS

In the workbook pages for each day, you will have an opportunity to reprogram a demand by applying one of the four methods of personal growth that are explained in *Handbook to Higher Consciousness*. Here is a short summary of each method:

1. **The Twelve Pathways.** The Twelve Pathways, which appear on the *inside front cover*, are a distillation of principles that human beings have used over the centuries—and have found enormously helpful in transforming their lives from the hopeless and helpless experience of being kicked around by circumstances. The pathways can guide you in your journey toward becoming a creative cause of unconditional love, effectiveness, and joy moment to moment. To get the most benefit, it is essential that you memorize them—for this helps instill them into both the conscious and unconscious areas of your brain. They'll be there when you most need them. The daily worksheets will tell you how to use the pathways and the other methods. Right now, turn to the inside front cover and slowly read the Twelve Pathways.

2. **The Centers of Consciousness.** Here are the centers that generate the way we react to life situations:

THREE SEPARATING CENTERS
1) **Security** (e.g., "If it happens I'll feel insecure.")
2) **Sensation** (e.g., "I need it to feel happy.")
3) **Power** (e.g., "I must forcefully control.")

FOUR UNIFYING CENTERS
4) **Love** ("I accept this emotionally.")
5) **Cornucopia** ("This adds abundance to my life.")
6) **Conscious-Awareness** (an impersonal perspective)
7) **Cosmic Consciousness** (a profound experience of understanding and unity)

When you clearly notice what is motivating your thoughts and actions in a given situation, you will find that these inner energies are coming from any of the seven centers. By learning to notice which center of consciousness your mind is operating from in each moment, you will give yourself more freedom to consciously choose the center you'll find most enjoyable—and most effective in handling situations. Take a look at the various emotions triggered in each center that are listed on the inside back cover.

3. **Link the Suffering With the Addictive Demand.** We find that our egos and minds really try to do the best they can in protecting us and helping us enjoy our lives. However, they're sometimes trapped in protecting demanding programs that are actually self-defeating. This method gives you practice in noticing how your unhappiness is linked with your demands. It encourages you to become aware of the various ways in which an addictive demand is bruising your life. We call those "ripoffs." You also identify illusory "payoffs" you think you are getting by holding on to a demand. This third method can gently and automatically help you uplevel an addictive demand to a preference. Please study pages 227 and 228 for ripoffs and payoffs.

4. **Consciousness Focusing.** This fourth method replaces a demanding program by using repetition to imprint on the mind a new preferential program that you would rather live with. Before using this method, we recommend that you reread Chapters 14 and 15 in *Handbook to Higher Consciousness* as a review. It will also be helpful to read Chapter 9 in *Gathering Power Through Insight and Love* by Ken and Penny Keyes.

To use the method of Consciousness Focusing, you simply repeat over and over a reprogramming phrase you have carefully chosen for yourself to help you replace the demanding programming that has been destroying your enjoyment and inner peace. In formulating a reprogramming phrase, be sure that your phrase:

1) Is specifically and directly related to your addictive demand. If your reprogramming phrase feels "right" but does not relate to your addictive demand, go back and reformulate your addictive demand.

2) Points you toward the image, thought, or feeling you most want.

3) Feels good to you; you can imagine having that experience.

4) Makes sense to your rational mind; intellectually you agree with it.

5) Is as pithy, rhythmic, and catchy as possible.

6) Is free from pressuring words such as "should," "shouldn't," "ought," or "I will."

7) Does not include such judgmental hooks as "I can love Melissa when she's bad."

When you have thoughtfully chosen a phrase that meets the above guidelines, you can repeat it 1,000 times a day until you feel it has replaced the old separating program in your mind that has been creating turmoil in your life. It can be helpful to keep track with a traffic counter.*

Be patient. Sometimes a reprogramming phrase will have a desired effect quite rapidly; sometimes it takes months—depending on how deeply the undesired programming is rooted in your conscious and unconscious mind.

---

*Traffic counters are available at most stationery stores, or you can order a counter (Item #800) from the Ken Keyes College Bookroom. (See pages 224 and 225 for ordering information.)

Getting the Most From This Workbook

We have suggested that you carefully read *Handbook to Higher Consciousness* and familiarize yourself with the methods, concepts, and terms which this workbook is based on. Occasionally reread it for a deeper and deeper understanding of the principles expressed. Memorizing the Twelve Pathways will help you benefit more from them.

By scheduling a time each day to use this workbook, you can make great strides in handling your demands and increasing your inner peace. The more time you spend on your inner growth, the faster you will get results. Divide the time you take between both pages of each day's practice.

The daily practice consists of four parts:

1. First you'll review your day by pinpointing the major demands that were triggered. Page 28 shows a sample worksheet.

    For each demand, note which center of consciousness you're in. You can tell this by the emotions you experience with the demand (see the inside back cover for a list of emotions under each center). Write down "1" for Security Center, "2" for Sensation Center, and/or "3" for Power Center. You could be in any or all of the first three centers while you run an addictive demand. Noting the center(s) of consciousness gives you an added perspective on your programming.

    Then choose any number of the Twelve Pathways (listed on the inside front cover) that you think will offer you insight into alternative ways you can respond internally. You can't choose a "wrong" pathway! *Say the entire pathway,* with thought as to how it may apply, before you write down its number. Allow approximately eight minutes for this section.

2. Next you will get practice in using one of the Living Love Methods presented in *Handbook to Higher Consciousness*. Allow at least five minutes for this part.

3. You'll write yourself a loving note of encouragement. Take a couple of minutes to write the note.

4. And finally, give yourself a great big hug! To some people, this may seem silly, but it can give your programming an important and meaningful message. Afterward put a check mark in the outlined heart—indicating that you actually hugged yourself.

The worksheets in the second and third months are the same as the first month. They will give you an opportunity to experience accelerated growth as you respond to the exercises on deeper levels. Many people have continued to benefit by repeating these exercises for a year or longer. If you do the practice long enough, your mind will get in the habit of catching addictive demands as they arise so they won't pile up and crystallize.

Handling Your Addictions

As you do the daily practice, you will be *handling* your addictions. This process puts you on the road of transformation. Handling your addictions is a simple three-step procedure:

1) Pinpointing a specific demand.
2) Taking intellectual responsibility (by acknowledging to yourself that your addictive demand is the immediate, practical cause of the separation you are feeling).
3) Using a method to begin bringing you an emotional freedom from the demand.

By using the form on the left-hand page of each day's worksheets to list your specifically pinpointed addictions, you begin to handle them. The rest of the practice session gives you an opportunity to further handle a demand by exploring the use of one of the four methods.

Trust your own experience after you handle your addiction. Even if you have not reprogrammed your addictive demand, by just doing the three things involved in handling your addiction, you will instantly begin to increase your creative insights and ability to love. And you can learn to run through these three mental steps in a minute or so whenever you need them!

Be patient with yourself as you use this workbook. Part of your journey is to witness the beauty and perfection of yourself, *right now*—exactly the way you are. You don't need to change yourself or uplevel a demand to a preference to be lovable—*you are lovable just as you are with all of your demands.*

The Living Love Methods can help you to love more and demand less. From time to time, review the worksheets you've filled in for any helpful insights that come to you. Remember: The main goals are to appreciate and love yourself here and now—just as you are—and then to share your love with those in your world. The more you give your love away, the more you'll have left!

You can *always* find something to appreciate about yourself. Here are some ways in which you may find yourself growing:

Being more honest with yourself or someone else.

Remembering that it is your addictive demand that causes your own separateness and unhappiness.

Being more aware of the robot-like demanding programming that has been controlling you.

Placing less blame on yourself and others.

Feeling the desire to love behind an addictive demand.

Asking for what you want.

Letting yourself experience your emotions more fully.

Letting go of an addictive demand more easily, and upleveling it to a preference.

Staying centered in a situation in which you used to get emotionally upset.

Feeling increasing acceptance, love, and happiness.

Realizing that love is contagious—and the more we give, the more we get.

Bringing "miracles" into your life that could only happen through the power of love.

Tips on Using the Daily Worksheets

1. In the first part of the daily practice session, note your addictive demands that your life has triggered.

2. Remember to make sure each demand is very specific. Check for the "4 W's:" Know *who* the demand is on, precisely *what* you want different, and *when* and *where* the demand got triggered. If you don't make your demands specific, you won't get as much out of this workbook.

3. After you write each addiction, identify the center of consciousness you were in: 1, 2, and/or 3 (Security, Sensation, and/or Power).

4. Then choose one or more pathways that seem most helpful to you with that demand. Be sure to say each one at least once, and write down the number of the pathway.

5. As you explore your emotional experience from day to day, you may discover addictive demands that you didn't realize you had. If that happens, take heart! Awareness is always a step forward. If some days go by without apparent demands being triggered, that's fine too. You can use those days' practices to work with demands from previous days or to chip away at some especially persistent ones that recur.

6. Acknowledge your growth and appreciate yourself. At the bottom of the last practice sheet for each day's session, there is space for you to write yourself a love note and acknowledge the ways in which you see your growth happening each day. Look for "wins" in how you handled your internal experience of the day. Give yourself positive strokes and encouragement—write to yourself as if you were your dearest, most perfect companion. You are! The more you can do this with yourself, the better you'll be able to give others genuine, loving support.

7. And, before you close the book each day, physically wrap your arms around yourself and give yourself the kind of compassionate, loving squeeze you would give to a child who you wanted to feel good. Hold yourself for ten seconds or so. Then put a check mark in the outlined heart indicating that you actually hugged yourself.

First
Month
of
Worksheets

1 SAMPLE PAGE

Date: _June 4_

I create the experience of	because my programming demands that	Cent. of Consc.	Path-way(s)
anger irritation	Tyler not have taken the car this morning without first talking to me.	3	12 1 9
★ disappointment frustration embarrassment	I have had enough money to buy Charlie a gift certificate to the health club for his birthday yesterday.	2 1	3 4 6 7
apprehension worry nervousness anxiety	Marcia not say she doesn't like my new advertising idea at the 4:00 meeting tomorrow.	1	2 5 10 11

The Twelve Pathways
Freeing Myself—Pathways 1, 2, and 3

"The Twelve Pathways to Higher Consciousness can show you how to accelerate your spiritual development and enable you to begin a new life of Living Love." **Handbook to Higher Consciousness**, Chapter 4.

1. I am freeing myself from security, sensation, and power addictions that make me try to forcefully control situations in my life and thus destroy my serenity and keep me from loving myself and others.
2. I am discovering how my consciousness-dominating addictions create my illusory version of the changing world of people and situations around me.
3. I welcome the opportunity (even if painful) that my minute-to-minute experience offers me to become aware of the addictions I must reprogram to be liberated from my robot-like emotional patterns.

★ For this practice, choose a demand you wrote above and put a star by it.

♥ Keeping the addictive demand in mind, open yourself to the inner wisdom you have for freeing yourself from addictive programming around that situation. To help you access that wisdom, say Pathways 1, 2, and 3 slowly and meditatively.

SAMPLE PAGE

✍ Write down your insights and experience while you were saying the first three pathways:

I noticed that saying the pathways had a calming effect on my mind. This situation, however disappointing and frustrating I make it, has something to teach me, especially when I welcome it as a chance to learn and grow. I can plan to spend my money differently in the future, and at the same time tell myself that loving Charlie is more important than anything I give him materially.

✍ Write how any of these three pathways could have assisted you during any other part of your day today:

When the orange juice spilled and dribbled down between the counter and the stove and I spent a long time cleaning it up, I could have used the 1st Pathway to help me keep my serenity and remember that what's important to me in each moment is to love or learn to love.

✍ Write three things you appreciate about yourself. They can be big or little appreciations. You are a lovable person!

1. *I am sincerely working on myself.*

2. *I have a willingness to learn new things.*

3. *I am sweet, caring, and motivated to make a difference for the better.*

♡ Give yourself a supportive, encouraging hug!

1

Make each demand specific with: who, what, when, and possibly where. See page 26 for tips on using your daily work pages.

Date: _____

I create the experience of	because my programming demands that	Cent. of Consc.	Path-way(s)

The Twelve Pathways
Freeing Myself—Pathways 1, 2, and 3

"The Twelve Pathways to Higher Consciousness can show you how to accelerate your spiritual development and enable you to begin a new life of Living Love." **Handbook to Higher Consciousness, Chapter 4.**

> 1. I am freeing myself from security, sensation, and power addictions that make me try to forcefully control situations in my life and thus destroy my serenity and keep me from loving myself and others.
> 2. I am discovering how my consciousness-dominating addictions create my illusory version of the changing world of people and situations around me.
> 3. I welcome the opportunity (even if painful) that my minute-to-minute experience offers me to become aware of the addictions I must reprogram to be liberated from my robot-like emotional patterns.

★ For this practice, choose an addictive demand you wrote above and put a star by it.

♥ Keeping the demand in mind, open yourself to the inner wisdom you have for freeing yourself from addictive programming around that situation. To help you access that wisdom, say Pathways 1, 2, and 3 slowly and meditatively.

✍ Write down your insights and experience while you were saying the first three pathways:

✍ Write how any of these three pathways could have assisted you during any other part of your day today:

✍ Write three things you appreciate about yourself. They can be big or little appreciations. You are a lovable person!

1.

2.

3.

♡ Give yourself a supportive, encouraging hug!

2

Make each demand specific with: who, what, when, and possibly where. See page 26 for tips on using your daily work pages.

Date: _____

I create the experience of	because my programming demands that	Cent. of Consc.	Path-way(s)

Centers of Consciousness
The Love Center

"As you learn to live more and more in the Love Center of Consciousness, you will begin to find that you are creating a new world in which your consciousness resides. People and conditions are no longer a threat to you—for no one can threaten your preferences." **Handbook to Higher Consciousness, Chapter 11.**

★ Put a star by the demand above with which you experienced the strongest separating emotions.

♥ Now use your imagination! In your mind, go back to the situation you wrote the addictive demand about. Take a deep breath, relax, and imagine your *emotional experience* being different. See and feel yourself experiencing love, inner peace, happiness, compassion, and *emotional* acceptance of yourself, the situation, and the people around you. You may want to include alternatives you can see when you use this love filter.

✍ Write a description of the Love Center experience you've just given yourself:

♥ REMEMBER: It's not what you say or do that creates the Love Center. It's how you feel inside! Learning how to say "no" from the Love Center really helps your life works better!

✍ You may have felt the Love Center as you wrote that description, or you may have said the words to yourself without feeling the love. Either way helps you to see there is a choice. Write yourself a love note, and list any insights and growth you perceive in your awareness today:

♡ Give yourself a Love Center hug!

33

3

Make each demand specific with: who, what, when, and possibly where. See page 26 for tips on using your daily work pages.

Date: _____

I create the experience of	because my programming demands that	Cent. of Consc.	Path-way(s)

Link the Suffering With the Addictive Demand
Practice in Pinpointing

"... the key to using the Third Method is to look deeply within yourself to find the emotion-backed demand that you are using to upset yourself. It's this simple. Just become more consciously conscious of the cause-effect relationship between your addictions and the resulting unhappiness, and you will be on the escalator that can take you directly to the Fourth Center of Consciousness." **Handbook to Higher Consciousness, Chapter 13.**

♥ In order to effectively link whatever unhappiness you are experiencing with an addictive demand, you need to know precisely what it is you're demanding. To help you do this, think of a repeating pattern in your life that you keep getting upset over.

✍ Briefly note the pattern:

♥ Put yourself back into the most recent situation as if it were happening right now. Answer briefly to yourself any of the following questions that seem to apply: What separating emotions am I feeling? What pain or tensions are in my body? What do my posture and face look like? What am I telling myself? Exactly what am I resisting in this situation? Or about myself? What threat does this person or situation represent to me? What is the worst that could happen? What is it about me that I think people can't love? What change am I demanding in order to feel happy and enough? Of myself? Of others?

✍ Write down any awarenesses or insights you gained of programming that was not previously apparent to you:

✍ Write down your addictive demand as clearly and precisely as you can pinpoint it:

I create the experience of _____

because my programming demands that _____

_____

_____

♥ This form reminds you that it is only the addictive programming in your mind that's causing your emotional experience, not the situation. Sometimes using the form is enough for you to uplevel an addictive demand to a preference. Sometimes further work is needed. Tomorrow, you can use another method on this demand to give you practice in reprogramming.

✍ Now write yourself a loving statement:

♡ And give yourself an encouraging hug!

35

4

Make each demand specific with: who, what, when, and possibly where. See page 26 for tips on using your daily work pages.

Date: _____

I create the experience of	because my programming demands that	Cent. of Consc.	Path-way(s)

Consciousness Focusing
Formulating Reprogramming Phrases

"Choose a reprogramming phrase that is short, pithy, and that feels good . . . that directly refers to the situation . . . ." **Handbook to Higher Consciousness**, Chapter 14.

✍ Rewrite the demand you worked with yesterday, or choose one from today that you're ready to work with because you linked your suffering to the addiction, and you *know* it's not only the situation that's causing you to feel upset:

I create the experience of _____

because my programming demands that _____

_____

♥ One of the best guidelines for forming a reprogramming phrase is to make a statement you want to live with and that you can imagine experiencing. Pick a beginning that feels possible and good. Here are some choices:

Beginning a Reprogramming Phrase	
I love . . .	I can choose to see myself as . . .
I can feel . . .	I have the right to . . .
I'm okay . . .	I can learn to accept . . .
I'm learning to love . . .	I'm willing to . . .

 Write several possible reprogramming phrases related to the demand:

★ Put a star by the phrase that you most strongly respond to with "Yes! That's what I want to tell myself!"

♥ Focus on the phrase. Close your eyes and breathe deeply. Let yourself relax and feel peaceful. As you begin to relax, repeat your phrase slowly and meditatively for several minutes.

 Remember, you can take that phrase with you into any situation where that or similar demands are triggered. Describe your experience of using the phrase:

 Write yourself a love note that reminds you of a way you are growing:

♡ Give yourself a hug!

37

5

Make each demand specific with: who, what, when, and possibly where. See page 26 for tips on using your daily work pages.

Date: _____

I create the experience of	because my programming demands that	Cent. of Consc.	Path-way(s)

Instant Consciousness Doubler
With Another Person

"The Instant Consciousness Doubler helps us realize that there are no 'others' in this world." **Handbook to Higher Consciousness, Chapter 16.**

♥ Think of a situation today in which your friend, relationship partner, or business associate really "got on your nerves." (If you can't think of a time today, scan back over the past week.)

✍ Briefly, describe what that person *actually* said or did. Avoid judgments or mind reading about his or her intentions:

✍ Recall a time you said or did or thought something similar. Write about that on the next page. If you can't think of such a time, imagine doing or thinking something similar:

✍ Get in touch with the place in you that feels loving and accepting toward yourself. Realize that the words, actions, or thoughts you used in the similar situation were based on your programming. Now, expand that love and acceptance to include the person you recently felt separate from. Write how it feels:

✍ Take a deep breath. Imagine that you are the other person with his/her programming. Put yourself in his/her shoes. Let yourself experience how you would have said or done exactly the same thing if you had his/her programming. Feel compassion for all of us acting like robots of our programming until we see that we have a choice. To increase your understanding, write what you might feel if you were in that other person's shoes:

✍ Write yourself a loving note. Write how you perceive yourself growing today:

♡ Give yourself a big hug!

39

6

Make each demand specific with: who, what, when, and possibly where. See page 26 for tips on using your daily work pages.

Date: _____

I create the experience of	because my programming demands that	Cent. of Consc.	Path-way(s)

Handling Your Addictions
Getting Specific With Your Demands

"Be very specific in pinpointing the demand. Exactly what do you want in that situation? What would you like to change in that situation? Tune in to your feelings and check to make sure you feel that you've pinpointed the demand which is causing your suffering." **Handbook to Higher Consciousness,** Chapter 14.

♥ Remember, what you've been doing each day is handling your addictions. "Handling" means three things: 1) pinpointing your specific demand, 2) taking intellectual responsibility (without blaming yourself), and 3) using a method.

★ To make sure you are pinpointing your demands as specifically as you can, put a star by one above, and write the answers to these questions:

✍ *Who* is the demand on?

✍ Exactly *what* are you demanding?

✍ *When* was it triggered?

✍ *Where* did the demand get triggered?

♥ Every time you pinpoint a demand, be sure you know what its "4 W's" are, even if the "when" and "where" are not written as part of the demand.

✍ Take intellectual responsibility without blaming yourself or anyone else. Write one sentence; e.g., "It's my addictive programming that creates this unhappiness, not the situation," or "I take responsibility for creating this suffering":

✍ Now use a method. Describe the same situation from the Conscious-Awareness Center. Write about yourself in the third person, nonjudgmentally observing what's happening inside and outside of you:

✍ You are lovable with every experience that your programming creates. Write a reminder to love yourself and to acknowledge the ways you've been growing:

♡ Remember that hug!

7

Make each demand specific with: who, what, when, and possibly where. See page 26 for tips on using your daily work pages.

Date: _____

I create the experience of	because my programming demands that	Cent. of Consc.	Path-way(s)

The Twelve Pathways
Being Here Now—Pathways 4, 5, and 6

"The world thus tends to be your mirror. A peaceful person lives in a peaceful world. An angry person creates an angry world. A helpful person generates helpful, loving energy in others." **Handbook to Higher Consciousness,** Chapter 6.

4. I always remember that I have everything I need to enjoy my here and now—unless I am letting my consciousness be dominated by demands and expectations based on the dead past or the imagined future.

5. I take full responsibility here and now for everything I experience, for it is my own programming that creates my actions and also influences the reactions of people around me.

6. I accept myself completely here and now and consciously experience everything I feel, think, say, and do (including my emotion-backed addictions) as a necessary part of my growth into higher consciousness.

♥ Think of a time during your day when you were not experiencing being "here and now" or when you judged or criticized yourself.

🖎 Write a brief description of how you felt:

♥ Say the Fourth, Fifth, and Sixth Pathways as you replay the incident in your mind. You may wish to say them more than once.

🖎 Write what you experienced as you mentally replayed the incident while saying Pathways 4, 5, and 6:

🖎 Write yourself a loving note and acknowledge the beauty that is in you right now:

♡ Give yourself a great BIG hug!

8

Make each demand specific with: who, what, when, and possibly where. See page 26 for tips on using your daily work pages.

Date: _____

I create the experience of	because my programming demands that	Cent. of Consc.	Path-way(s)

Centers of Consciousness
Imagining ... the Fifth Center

"... you will begin to feel that you live in a friendly world that will always give you 'enough' when you live in the higher Centers of Consciousness. ... your world is perfect from the point of view of continually providing you with precisely the life experiences that you need for your overall development as a conscious being." Handbook to Higher Consciousness, Chapter 11.

★ Put a star by a demand above in which you felt particularly caught in the Security, Sensation, or Power Center of Consciousness.

♥ Imagine that situation is happening right now. Use your imagination to experience the Fifth Center—*Cornucopia*. This center emphasizes the gentleness or intensity of the lesson, appreciation that you created the lesson with the particular people involved, and/or welcoming the lesson and the opportunity for growth.

✐ Write how you could experience the situation as a lesson which is part of the abundance of your life:

✐ Now, imagine that you are in the same situation as it happened. Instead of creating separating emotions, you create joy, wonder, and a feeling of having more than you need to be happy. Write how you could experience that situation by appreciating the "cornucopia" life is offering you:

> ✐ Be gentle with yourself! If you can *see* the "strawberries" (the things in your life to appreciate) yet not *feel* appreciation, that's okay. Enjoy yourself with whatever you feel. Write yourself a note about the strawberries of being you:
>
> ♡ Feel the pleasure of loving yourself and put it into a hug!

45

9

Make each demand specific with: who, what, when, and possibly where. See page 26 for tips on using your daily work pages.

Date: _____

I create the experience of	because my programming demands that	Cent. of Consc.	Path-way(s)

Link the Suffering With the Addictive Demand
Exploring Ripoffs

"You make a giant step toward higher consciousness when you become fully aware of the price in happiness you must pay for each addiction." **Handbook to Higher Consciousness**, Chapter 4.

♥ In order to make the connection that it is your addictive demand that's basically causing your unhappiness (not you, other people, or events), you must first be aware of how your programming is penalizing you—like a hidden dagger inside you!

★ Choose a demand from above and put a star by it.

♥ Turn to page 227 listing ripoffs. Examine the many areas and ways in which demands diminish your happiness.

🕭 In the following list, circle the ways this addiction is hurting you. Add words to make the list specific to your addiction; e.g., *where* is your body tense? From *whom* are you feeling separate?

1. Body reactions: tension, constricted breath, rapid heartbeat...

2. Emotions: fear, frustration, anger...

3. Attitude toward self: low self-esteem...

4. Attitude toward others: judgmental, inability to feel close...

5. Energy, time: low, lost, wasted...

6. Perception of what is happening in life: distorted, illusory, inability to see surrounding beauty...

7. Spontaneity, creativity, openness: compulsive, inflexible, blocked...

8. Humor: no humor, serious problem, worried face...

9. Cooperative relationships with other people: triggering others' addictions...

10. Alternatives and choices: limited perspective, "tunnel vision"...

11. Making changes: limited ability due to wasted energy and lack of insight...

12. Enjoying your life: not enough, protecting and defending...

♥ All of these ripoffs are basically caused by your demand. Avoid blaming your upset feelings on someone else, a situation, or what you said or did. *Blame your programming—NOT YOU!* Sometimes, becoming aware of how that demand makes you upset is all that you need to be willing to uplevel the demand to a preference. At other times, you may choose to hold on to the addictive demand. You can love yourself either way!

✍ Now write yourself a loving note and remind yourself of the growing awareness you experienced today:

♡ Give yourself a hug!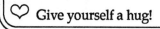

10

Make each demand specific with: who, what, when, and possibly where. See page 26 for tips on using your daily work pages.

Date: _____

I create the experience of	because my programming demands that	Cent. of Consc.	Path-way(s)

Consciousness Focusing
Using a Phrase with Energy

"When you see clearly that it is your addiction that is immediately causing your suffering and not the situation in itself, and when you see how unnecessary it is to make the demands you have been making, then you are ready to start reprogramming." **Handbook to Higher Consciousness**, Chapter 14.

♥ Use Consciousness Focusing when you want inner peace, love, and freedom from your addictive programming *more* than you want what you are demanding.

★ Put a star by an addictive demand above that you feel you are ready to uplevel to a preference. (If you're not ready to uplevel any of today's demands, pick one you can imagine wanting to uplevel.)

48

✍ Sometimes it takes formulating several phrases before you find one that feels right. Come up with ones that feel good and that energize you. Using the seven guidelines on page 21, write at least five reprogramming phrases related to the demand you chose:

★ Put a star by the reprogramming phrase that feels best to you.

♥ Visualize the incident in which you triggered the demand. Realize that with motivation to get free of the addictive programming, you can have inner peace instead of emotional turmoil. With added intensity, say one of your reprogramming phrases silently or aloud, over and over for several minutes.

✍ Write how it felt to use that phrase:

♥ Use this phrase tomorrow while you are walking, jogging, or doing any kind of physical activity.

✍ Write yourself a loving reprogramming phrase below, and say it softly to yourself several times right now:

♥ I am ♥
lovable...

♡ Give yourself a tender hug.

11

Make each demand specific with: who, what, when, and possibly where. See page 26 for tips on using your daily work pages.

Date: _____

I create the experience of	because my programming demands that	Cent. of Consc.	Path-way(s)

Addictive and Preferential Programming

"Every addiction leaves us vulnerable; preferences enable us to continually enjoy life. When our biocomputers operate from preferential programming, our happiness is not affected—regardless of whether the outside world fits our preferences or not." **Handbook to Higher Consciousness,** Appendix 1.

♥ We can more or less enjoy our day when things go the way we want. When things don't go the way we want, our internal experience depends on whether our programmed response is addictive or preferential.

♥ Scan your day for situations you reacted to with addictive programming. You know an addiction has been triggered if 1) you feel separating emotions, 2) you feel body tension, 3) your rational mind keeps churning over the same thing, or 4) your life seems bogged down by a problem. You can use the above addictive demands to help you with this perspective of your day.

✍ Outline these situations in six words or less, such as "My car wouldn't start":

♥ Now shift into an awareness of the times today when you reacted with preferential programming to situations you didn't like. These incidents can be less obvious than the ones you get upset about since our minds don't snag on them. Yet noticing how much preferential programming we already have can be refreshing feedback. Realizing how much you're already winning can inspire you to keep on winning! Recall from your day the moments when you felt emotionally peaceful, your body felt relaxed, and your mind did not get stuck on a tape loop— even when things did not go as you would have liked.

✍ List those times here:

✍ Write yourself a gentle note and remind yourself that you are beautiful, capable, and lovable just the way you are:

♡ Hug yourself with compassion for both your addictive and preferential programming.

12

Make each demand specific with: who, what, when, and possibly where. See page 26 for tips on using your daily work pages.

Date: _____

I create the experience of	because my programming demands that	Cent. of Consc.	Path-way(s)

Combining Methods
Pathways; Centers of Consciousness

"Because you have created a beautiful, peaceful world in which you now live, you are helping everyone around you find the beautiful, peaceful place inside. And you can accept help without feeling that an obligation is created." **Handbook to Higher Consciousness, Chapter 11.**

✍ Which pathways that you chose above had the most meaning for you? Write down particular insights you got from saying them:

✍ On the next page, write a brief description of an incident today in which you created separating emotions:

✍Now rewrite the scene, imagining that you experience it from the Love Center:

✍ Rewrite the scene again, this time with the sense of abundance and opportunity for growth that comes from the Cornucopia Center:

✍ Write down the "wins" you had today in your consciousness growth:

♡ Hug yourself!

13

Make each demand specific with: who, what, when, and possibly where. See page 26 for tips on using your daily work pages.

Date: _____

I create the experience of	because my programming demands that	Cent. of Consc.	Path-way(s)

The Twelve Pathways
Interacting With Others—Pathways 7, 8, and 9

"Everyone and everything around you is your teacher." **Handbook to Higher Consciousness,** Chapter 5.

7. I open myself genuinely to all people by being willing to fully communicate my deepest feelings, since hiding in any degree keeps me stuck in my illusion of separateness from other people.

8. I feel with loving compassion the problems of others without getting caught up emotionally in their predicaments that are offering them messages they need for their growth.

9. I act freely when I am tuned in, centered, and loving, but if possible I avoid acting when I am emotionally upset and depriving myself of the wisdom that flows from love and expanded consciousness.

★ Put a star by a demand above that was on someone else. Say that demand, then the Seventh Pathway, the same demand again, then the Eighth Pathway, the demand once again, and then the Ninth Pathway.

✍ Write what you experienced as you alternated the demand with those three pathways:

✍ Write how you might have felt or acted differently if the insights reflected in Pathways 7, 8, and 9 had been in your consciousness at the time the demand was triggered:

✍ Enjoy the journey! Write yourself an encouraging note about the "wins" you've had today in your consciousness growth:

♡ Give yourself a reassuring hug!
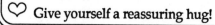

14

Make each demand specific with: who, what, when, and possibly where. See page 26 for tips on using your daily work pages.

Date: _____

I create the experience of	because my programming demands that	Cent. of Consc.	Path-way(s)

Centers of Consciousness
Watching From the Sixth Center

"It is liberating to have a Center from which your Conscious-awareness watches your body and mind perform on the lower five centers." **Handbook to Higher Consciousness,** Chapter 9.

✍ Stop the movie of your day by focusing on one incident in which you triggered separating emotions. Give a two- or three-sentence description of what happened in that scene:

♥ Take a deep breath. Now, mentally step back from the situation and create the drama using the Conscious-Awareness Center. You are now an impartial observer, watching and not identifying with the character (using "she" or "he" instead of "I") in the drama. Witness the scene moment by moment without judging, analyzing, generalizing, or labeling what is happening.

✍ Write a description of the scene using the Sixth Center. Remember: NO JUDGMENTS!

✍ You're doing fine! Appreciate yourself for continuing to use the workbook. Write any insights you got today:

♡ And give yourself a great big loving hug!

15

Make each demand specific with: who, what, when, and possibly where. See page 26 for tips on using your daily work pages.

Date: _____

I create the experience of	because my programming demands that	Cent. of Consc.	Path-way(s)

Link the Suffering With the Addictive Demand
Exploring Payoffs

"Changes leading to happiness come most rapidly when you can fully engage both your ego and rational mind (two of your most powerful faculties) in the game of helping you eliminate each addiction." **Handbook to Higher Consciousness,** Chapter 13.

♥ Each time you hold on to an addiction, there is a real or imaginary "payoff" you think you'll get. Identifying and questioning the value of these payoffs will help you to be aware of why your programming is hanging on to that demand.

★ Put a star by a demand pinpointed above.

✍ Using the list that follows as a general guide, check the payoffs you think you get by holding on to your demands and those emotions. Add specific details; e.g., who will give you attention, which other addictions you get to avoid confronting:

❑ Get to be right, feel superior.

❑ Get attention, sympathy, comfort, agreement, camaraderie.

❑ Avoid taking responsibility for how I feel. I can blame_____

❑ Get to avoid confronting other addictions. _____

- ❏ People won't think I'm _____
- ❏ Excuse for poor performance; people won't reject me.
- ❏ People will know I'm a good _____
- ❏ Feels safe and familiar.
- ❏ Feels safe to keep a distance from _____
- ❏ Get to play martyr and/or the victim role.
- ❏ Get to enjoy the fantasy.
- ❏ Get to feel close to others who have the same addictions. _____
- ❏ Feel a sense of intensity and aliveness.
- ❏ I/he/she will change. _____
- ❏ They'll make it up to me. _____

★ Which one do you feel is the strongest? Put a star by that payoff.

✍ Focusing on that payoff, check any insights you have about the supposed payoff that makes you hold on to your addiction:

- ❏ It's an illusion; I don't really get that payoff.
- ❏ "What is" doesn't change by holding on to the addiction.
- ❏ When I get this payoff it lasts only temporarily and doesn't bring continued peace and happiness.
- ❏ It's not enough.
- ❏ Getting this payoff doesn't feel as good as love.
- ❏ I create more separateness in my life.
- ❏ I lose out on the fullness of what is available in my life. I cut down on my involvement.
- ❏ I solidify my judgmental opinions by holding on.
- ❏ I'm setting up my next lesson.
- ❏ I can put energy into getting or enjoying that "payoff" from a preferential space.
- ❏ I can go for that payoff directly; e.g., ask for attention, choose to change something in my life.
- ❏ Other insights:

✍ Be patient with yourself. You are growing in awareness. Write yourself some loving thoughts in a note:

♡ Give yourself a warm hug.

16

Make each demand specific with: who, what, when, and possibly where. See page 26 for tips on using your daily work pages.

Date: _____

I create the experience of	because my programming demands that	Cent. of Consc.	Path-way(s)

Consciousness Focusing
Intensive Mode

"But it's your determination and will to be free of the addiction that really accomplishes the reprogramming...." **Handbook to Higher Consciousness,** Chapter 14.

♥ Using the Intensive Mode of Consciousness Focusing may bring about a fast and dramatic shift in your programming.

★ Put a star by an addictive demand above in which intense heavy emotions are involved, about which you have become keenly aware of its ripoffs, *and* that you feel you're ready to uplevel to a preference. (If none of the demands above fit that description, find a previous days' demand and rewrite it.)

✍ Write several reprogramming phrases, using the seven guidelines on page 21."

★ Put a star by the one that makes the strongest impact on your positive energies.

♥ Find a place where you can be by yourself to focus on the phrase. Review the ripoffs of the demand. Keeping them in mind, build up a strong determination to be free of the old programming. Start silently saying the phrase in your head, and tense your muscles. Allow intensity to build and let yourself experience whatever emotions come up. After you repeat the phrase as long as you want, keep your eyes closed and review the same situation, this time with your new phrase running silently in your head.

✍ Appreciate yourself for the freedom you are giving yourself. Write a note acknowledging ways you experienced an increase in your love today:

♡ Give yourself a hug!

17

Make each demand specific with: who, what, when, and possibly where. See page 26 for tips on using your daily work pages.

Date: _____

I create the experience of	because my programming demands that	Cent. of Consc.	Path-way(s)

Instant Consciousness Doubler
With Yourself

"We have at all times been lovable. A child may be naughty, but he is always lovable. And so we are all children as long as we are programmed with our lower consciousness addictions." **Handbook to Higher Consciousness,** Chapter 3.

✍ Focus on a time today when you felt something other than love or acceptance for yourself, when you told yourself you should have been different. Write what you felt and what you did that triggered the feeling:

✍ Take a deep breath. Write the name of someone you deeply love, respect, or admire:

♥ Imagine that he/she said or did what you said or did when you created that separation. Feel yourself loving and accepting him or her doing something similar.

✍ Write how that would feel. Perhaps you'd like to include what you might say to him or her with this loving feeling:

♥ Now, expand that love and compassion to include yourself. Give yourself the same understanding and acceptance that you give this other person. Remember that in your essence you are not your thoughts, actions, or programming.

✍ Write what you might tell yourself with the increased understanding and acceptance you deserve:

✍ Write yourself a loving, compassionate note:

♡ Give yourself some love with a BIG hug!

18

Make each demand specific with: who, what, when, and possibly where. See page 26 for tips on using your daily work pages.

Date: _____

I create the experience of	because my programming demands that	Cent. of Consc.	Path-way(s)

Combining Methods
Link the Suffering; Consciousness Focusing

"We learn to love others by accepting and loving ourselves—and vice versa." Handbook to Higher Consciousness, Chapter 8.

★ Choose the most persistent addictive demand above and put a star by it.

✍ List several ways that your demand penalizes you:

✍ Formulate several possible reprogramming phrases related to the demand. Write ones that feel good, that you would like to instill in your mind, and that you can imagine experiencing as a reality for you:

★ Choose the phrase that feels most energizing to you and put a star by it.

♥ Now, keeping in mind all the ways the addictive demand has ripped you off, repeat your reprogramming phrase over and over for several minutes with a determination to free yourself from the addiction.

✍ Take a deep breath and write yourself a note that's filled with joy and a sense of inner peace!

♡ And remember that hug!

19

Make each demand specific with: who, what, when, and possibly where. See page 26 for tips on using your daily work pages.

Date: _____

I create the experience of	because my programming demands that	Cent. of Consc.	Path-way(s)

The Twelve Pathways
Discovering My Conscious-Awareness—Pathways 10, 11, and 12

"We're just not that different from each other." **Handbook to Higher Consciousness**, Chapter 8.

---

10. I am continually calming the restless scanning of my rational mind in order to perceive the finer energies that enable me to unitively merge with everything around me.
11. I am constantly aware of which of the Seven Centers of Consciousness I am using, and I feel my energy, perceptiveness, love, and inner peace growing as I open all of the Centers of Consciousness.
12. I am perceiving everyone, including myself, as an awakening being who is here to claim his or her birthright to the higher consciousness planes of unconditional love and oneness.

✍ Think of a time today when your mind was striving for, clinging to, or rejecting something or someone. Briefly describe what you were telling yourself (continue writing on next page):

♥ Keeping that experience in mind, say Pathways 10, 11, and 12 slowly and meditatively. Do this several times.

✍ Write whatever happened inside you as you said those three pathways; e.g., insights, times when your mind wandered, calmness, resistance, new awareness:

♥ Say the Twelfth Pathway again as a reminder to accept yourself.

✍ Write yourself a note filled with love, and acknowledge the "wins" you had today in your consciousness growth:

♡ Give yourself a great big hug!

20

Make each demand specific with: who, what, when, and possibly where. See page 26 for tips on using your daily work pages.

Date: _____

I create the experience of	because my programming demands that	Cent. of Consc.	Path-way(s)

Centers of Consciousness
Playing Through the Various Centers

"One of the benefits of the seven-step consciousness scale is to enable you to see your drama from a perspective so that you can choose the filters you wish to use in generating your experience." **Handbook to Higher Consciousness,** Chapter 9.

✍ Write a brief, objective description of an incident in which you triggered separating emotions:

✍ Use your imagination to write a possible scenario of that same scene from each of the centers of consciousness below. Write which emotions you would feel; the thoughts that would be in your head; and, if you want, the possible actions that would come from those thoughts and emotions:

SECURITY:

SENSATION:

POWER:

LOVE:

CORNUCOPIA:

CONSCIOUS-AWARENESS:

✍ Notice any insights and shifts in perspective you got today, and give yourself some love in a note:

♡ Choose the Love or Cornucopia Center from which to hug yourself!

21

Make each demand specific with: who, what, when, and possibly where. See page 26 for tips on using your daily work pages.

Date: _____

I create the experience of	because my programming demands that	Cent. of Consc.	Path-way(s)

Link the Suffering With the Addictive Demand
Weighing Ripoffs and Payoffs

" 'Have I suffered enough?' " **Handbook to Higher Consciousness,** Chapter 13.

♥ When you first become aware of an addiction, you may not experience that you are suffering much. You also may feel that the payoffs for holding on are great. As you gain awareness of ripoffs and payoffs, you will begin to feel the real price you pay for holding on to your addiction and to realize that the reward in the payoffs is very scant.

★ Put a star by the heaviest addictive demand above.

♥ Turn to pages 227 and 228. Review the ripoffs and payoffs listed.

✍ Briefly list your ripoffs and payoffs on the next page. Use one to five words, such as "tension in neck," "frustration," and "I get to be right":

70

_____	_____
_____	_____
_____	_____
_____	_____
_____	_____
_____	_____
_____	_____
_____	_____
_____	_____
_____	_____
_____	_____
_____	_____

✖ Put an "x" by each payoff you see as *illusory* (you don't actually get it by holding on to the demand) or *temporary* (you get temporary pleasure but it's not enough).

♥ Look at the balance of ripoffs and payoffs. Is the demand worth holding on to? Holding on to the demand—even with those payoffs—perpetuates isolation, crystallizes opinions, and prolongs suffering. You lose involvement, wisdom, and love.

> ✍ Write an acknowledgment of the beauty and perfection of your process of growth in a "mushy" love note to yourself:
>
>
>
>
>
>
> ♡ Hug yourself just for being you!

22

Make each demand specific with: who, what, when, and possibly where. See page 26 for tips on using your daily work pages.

Date: _____

I create the experience of	because my programming demands that	Cent. of Consc.	Path-way(s)

Consciousness Focusing
The Catalyst

"The Catalyst ALL WAYS US LIVING LOVE can be slowly and silently repeated to enable you to continuously tune in to that part of you that does not see others as him, her, *or* them—but always us." **Handbook to Higher Consciousness, Chapter 13.**

♥ You can use a general reprogramming phrase as a foreground figure against which your feelings, thoughts, and actions are the background. "All Ways Us Living Love" is a general phrase that we call the "Catalyst." You can use this phrase to help calm your mind when it's overloaded with addictive programming and thereby make room for understanding with your heart.

♥ Look over the demands you listed on the previous page. Recall the various situations today in which you felt emotionally triggered. Close your eyes and breathe deeply. Let yourself relax. Begin saying "All Ways Us Living Love," emphasizing a subsequent word each time. As you repeat the Catalyst slowly and meditatively for several minutes, allow your mind to reflect on those situations today, and imagine being back in them—this time feeling calm and peaceful.

✍ Describe your experience of using the Catalyst:

✍ Write down the "wins" you have recently had in your consciousness growth:

♡ Give yourself a great BIG hug!

23

Make each demand specific with: who, what, when, and possibly where. See page 26 for tips on using your daily work pages.

Date: _____

I create the experience of	because my programming demands that	Cent. of Consc.	Path-way(s)

The Law of Higher Consciousness

"Love everyone unconditionally—including yourself.
This law can enable you to find the hidden splendor within yourself and others." **Handbook to Higher Consciousness**, Chapter 3.

✍ List some of the times today when you could have applied the Law of Higher Consciousness, but didn't. Remember that the law includes appreciating and loving yourself unconditionally:

Describe what those times might have been like if your programming had allowed you to love unconditionally:

 You are absolutely lovable just the way you are! Write yourself an encouraging note:

♡ And give yourself a loving, tender hug!

24

Make each demand specific with: who, what, when, and possibly where. See page 26 for tips on using your daily work pages.

Date: _____

I create the experience of	because my programming demands that	Cent. of Consc.	Path-way(s)

Combining Methods
Centers of Consciousness; Doubler; Catalyst

". . . you experience the power, the deep peace, and the exquisite beauty of letting your energy harmonize with the energies around you." **Handbook to Higher Consciousness, Chapter 12.**

★ Put a star by a demand you wrote above.

✍ Describe that incident from the Conscious-Awareness Center. Refer to yourself in the third person, nonjudgmentally witnessing your inner thoughts and feelings, and the outer actions of yourself and others:

✍ Now move into the Cornucopia Center. Describe the scene as it would be experienced with joy, gratitude, richness, and wonder:

✍ Now look at the person you felt separate from (yourself or someone else) through compassionate eyes. Understand that this person's behavior is a reflection of inner programming that may be trapping him or her in feeling upset. Realize that this person is doing his/her best to make his/her life work and to feel loved and loving. Write about this person from such a perspective:

✍ Keep the Catalyst, "All Ways Us Living Love," in the back of your mind as you write yourself a note. Give yourself credit for the ways you are opening yourself to more love in your life:

♡ Appreciate yourself with a hug!

77

25

Make each demand specific with: who, what, when, and possibly where. See page 26 for tips on using your daily work pages.

Date: _____

I create the experience of	because my programming demands that	Cent. of Consc.	Path-way(s)

The Twelve Pathways
All Twelve Pathways

"One interesting aspect of the Twelve Pathways is that if you can follow any one of them completely on the deeper levels, you will be using almost all of them." Handbook to Higher Consciousness, Chapter 6.

♥ Focus on the hardest time for you today. Recall the physical sensations and separating emotions you felt. Remember what thoughts went through your mind.

♥ As you stay focused on that time, say each of the Twelve Pathways with emphasis and expression.

✍ Write what changes happened in your **physical sensations**:

✍ Write what happened with your **emotional experience** as you said the pathways:

✍ Write what **insights** came to your mind:

✍ Write yourself a loving note and acknowledge how you see yourself growing today:

♡ Give yourself a BIG hug!

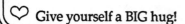

26

Make each demand specific with: who, what, when, and possibly where. See page 26 for tips on using your daily work pages.

Date: _____

I create the experience of	because my programming demands that	Cent. of Consc.	Path-way(s)

Centers of Consciousness
Fourth, Fifth, and Sixth Centers

"A beautiful aspect of the consciousness scale is that each time you go up a step in the scale, your life gives you: 1. More energy. 2. More contact with people. 3. More enjoyment." **Handbook to Higher Consciousness**, Chapter 9.

★ Put a star by a demand above.

♥ Relax. Focus on the situation in which you created that demand, keeping in mind that the events stay the same. Imagine changing your emotional experience by using preferential programming. Re-create that scene in your mind and describe it:

✍ Through the **Love Center:**

✍ Through the **Cornucopia Center:**

✍ Through the **Conscious-Awareness Center:**

✍ Whatever is happening inside you is perfect for your enjoyment and/or your growth and openness to love. Write what you appreciate in your life today—including what you appreciate about yourself:

♡ Hug yourself!

27

Make each demand specific with: who, what, when, and possibly where. See page 26 for tips on using your daily work pages.

Date: _____

I create the experience of	because my programming demands that	Cent. of Consc.	Path-way(s)

Link the Suffering With the Addictive Demand
Comparing Ripoffs of a Demand With Benefits of a Preference

"In other words, with Preferential Programming, there is no way I can 'lose' and there is definitely a way that I can 'win.' " **Handbook to Higher Consciousness,** Chapter 23.

★ Put a star by a demand above that you would like to work with further.

✍ With this demand in mind, circle in the first column on the next page all the ways that this demand is keeping you from enjoying your life. Add any other details not listed:

✍ Now circle all the items in the second column that indicate the benefits you may receive when you successfully uplevel this demand to a preference. Add any other details that come to mind:

82

	Ripoffs of This Demand	Benefits of a Preference
Body	body tense, weak, constricted breath, rapid heartbeat,	body relaxed, breath normal, heartbeat normal,
Emotions	fear, frustration, anger,	acceptance, peace, love, happiness,
Attitude toward self	low self-esteem, limited feeling of love, judgmentalness,	high self-esteem, self-appreciation, emotional acceptance of self,
Attitude toward others	inability to feel close, limited love, criticalness,	emotional acceptance of others, closeness, love,

♥ Close your eyes and for a minute imagine what you will be doing and saying when this demand becomes a preference. Experience the differences between demanding and preferring.

✍ Write the ways you see yourself growing and opening up:

♡ Lovingly embrace yourself!

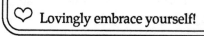

83

28

Date: _____

I create the experience of	because my programming demands that	Cent. of Consc.	Path-way(s)

Consciousness Focusing
Reprogramming Phrases for Core Beliefs

"Your predictions and expectations are thus self-fulfilling. Since your consciousness creates your universe, all you have to do to change your world is to change your consciousness!" **Handbook to Higher Consciousness, Chapter 6.**

♥ We all base our experience of life on beliefs and assumptions, some of which are beneficial and some of which are self-destructive. We can change self-defeating core beliefs when we recognize them as programming rather than "reality" carved in stone or "just the way things are." One way to explore possible self-defeating core beliefs is to look for repeating patterns in the addictive demands we trigger day to day.

♥ Looking at the demands above, choose one, and explore what general attitudes might lie behind that demand. For example, if you create the experience of frustration and annoyance because your programming demands that you not eat a whole bag of tortilla chips at lunch today, perhaps you have a core belief that says "I can't be trusted to take care of myself," or maybe it's "I have

to be thin to be lovable." Examples of other core beliefs are "No matter how hard I try, it's never good enough," "Men (or women) will leave sooner or later," and "People don't want to listen to me."

✍ Based on your demand, write out what some of your self-defeating thoughts or assumptions might be:

♥ You can come up with your own reprogramming phrases to challenge a self-destructive core belief and create a perception you'd like to experience; e.g., "Mother is doing the best she can and I can feel at peace with her," "I deserve to enjoy my life," or "I'm learning to feel beautiful, capable, and lovable."

✍ Write out phrases that if used enough might free you from the possible self-defeating patterns you wrote above:

★ Select the phrase that feels best to you right now and put a star by it. Say the phrase 1,000 times tomorrow, using a counter as described on page 21.

> ✍ Write a note reminding yourself of ways you are lovable:
>
>
> ♡ Show yourself some love with a hug!

29

Make each demand specific with: who, what, when, and possibly where. See page 26 for tips on using your daily work pages.

Date: _____

I create the experience of	because my programming demands that	Cent. of Consc.	Path-way(s)

Instant Consciousness Doubler
With Another Person

"The love you have for yourself and the love you have for 'another' are building blocks joining together within you to create the beautiful edifice of real love." Handbook to Higher Consciousness, Chapter 3.

✍ Select a time today when you felt angry, afraid, resentful, or disgusted with someone else. Write what he or she did or said when you triggered those emotions:

✍ Increase your love and compassion for that person. Imagine what might have been his/her internal thoughts or feelings behind the words or actions today. Write them down:

♥ Remember that it's not that person's essential being that you felt separate from, but rather the things he or she was saying or doing—which was simply coming from programming. Your programming didn't like his/her programming!

✍ Write how this perspective can alter your experience of this person:

✍ Write a note to remind yourself of the beauty and perfection of you, just the way you are:

♡ Give yourself a great big hug!

30

The Highest Happiness

"You will increase your growth into higher consciousness by learning to flow energy into meeting the needs of 'others' as though they were your own needs." Handbook to Higher Consciousness, Chapter 11.

♥ As you increase your skill in handling security, sensation, and power center demands, you will discover a rise in energy, insight, appreciation for yourself and others, and happiness in your life. As you become richer and richer in happiness, you will find it increasingly satisfying to open your heart with more generosity. You can be more generous with your time to help others, with your emotional love and support, with the money that flows into your life, and with your possessions. Such inner richness will make you want to do more and more to help other people.

✍ In the space below, briefly write how you may choose to do something for someone (other than yourself) next week without any expectation that the person would "pay you back" or return your generosity in any way:

Suggestions to Spark Your Ideas

1. Buy a delicious snack and take it to a neighbor for no special reason.

2. Offer to help with something that you usually do not volunteer aid with.

3. Straighten up a room in your house in which you did not make the mess.

4. Show some extra love and caring for someone who seems upset, angry, or depressed.

5. Write a note of appreciation for someone you have felt separate from.

6. Volunteer your time with a worthy nonprofit organization such as Red Cross, Senior Citizen Center, or Women's Crisis Center.

7. Tithe 10% of your income to a civic or spiritual organization.

8. Take a few minutes to talk or play with a child with whom you usually don't spend time.

9. Go to the home of an elderly person and ask if you can help him/her for an hour in any way he/she could use it.

10. Carry a bag of canned food to a minister, priest, or rabbi and ask him/her to give it to a needy family.

11. Get some flowers and leave them by the front door of someone you don't know. Can you do it anonymously?

12. Write in some of your own ideas:

"...loving and serving yields the maximum of all the beautiful things that life can offer." Handbook to Higher Consciousness, Chapter 11.

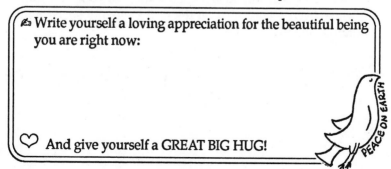

✍ Write yourself a loving appreciation for the beautiful being you are right now:

♡ And give yourself a GREAT BIG HUG!

31

Make each demand specific with: who, what, when, and possibly where. See page 26 for tips on using your daily work pages.

Date: _____

I create the experience of	because my programming demands that	Cent. of Consc.	Path-way(s)

Creating Your Own
You Are the Author of the Drama of Your Life . . .
and of This Practice Sheet!

"You have everything you need to work on yourself and you can positively reprogram yourself to eliminate all the hellish emotions that keep you from enjoying your life continuously." **Handbook to Higher Consciousness,** Chapter 15.

♥ Give thought to all the methods you have been using this past month. Is there one that seems especially liberating for you? Create your own way to bring a sparkle into your day with a method. Write your idea on the next page and spend a few minutes actually doing it.

♥ You can enjoy watching the movie of your life!

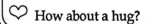 Congratulations for staying with a daily practice for 31 days! Now choose the kind of loving note that you want to write today:

♡ How about a hug?

Second Month of Worksheets

1

Make each demand specific with: who, what, when, and possibly where. See page 26 for tips on using your daily work pages.

Date: _____

I create the experience of	because my programming demands that	Cent. of Consc.	Path-way(s)

The Twelve Pathways
Freeing Myself—Pathways 1, 2, and 3

"The Twelve Pathways to Higher Consciousness can show you how to accelerate your spiritual development and enable you to begin a new life of Living Love." Handbook to Higher Consciousness, Chapter 4.

1. I am freeing myself from security, sensation, and power addictions that make me try to forcefully control situations in my life and thus destroy my serenity and keep me from loving myself and others.
2. I am discovering how my consciousness-dominating addictions create my illusory version of the changing world of people and situations around me.
3. I welcome the opportunity (even if painful) that my minute-to-minute experience offers me to become aware of the addictions I must reprogram to be liberated from my robot-like emotional patterns.

★ For this practice, choose an addictive demand you wrote above and put a star by it.

♥ Keeping the demand in mind, open yourself to the inner wisdom you have for freeing yourself from addictive programming around that situation. To help you access that wisdom, say Pathways 1, 2, and 3 slowly and meditatively.

✍ Write down your insights and experience while you were saying the first three pathways:

✍ Write how any of these three pathways could have assisted you during any other part of your day today:

✍ Write three things you appreciate about yourself. They can be big or little appreciations. You are a lovable person!

1.

2.

3.

♡ Give yourself a supportive, encouraging hug!

95

2

Make each demand specific with: who, what, when, and possibly where. See page 26 for tips on using your daily work pages.

Date: _____

I create the experience of	because my programming demands that	Cent. of Consc.	Path-way(s)

Centers of Consciousness
The Love Center

"As you learn to live more and more in the Love Center of Consciousness, you will begin to find that you are creating a new world in which your consciousness resides. People and conditions are no longer a threat to you—for no one can threaten your preferences." **Handbook to Higher Consciousness,** Chapter 11.

★ Put a star by the demand above with which you experienced the strongest separating emotions.

♥ Now use your imagination! In your mind, go back to the situation you wrote the addictive demand about. Take a deep breath, relax, and imagine your *emotional experience* being different. See and feel yourself experiencing love, inner peace, happiness, compassion, and *emotional* acceptance of yourself, the situation, and the people around you. You may want to include alternatives you can see when you use this love filter.

96

✍ Write a description of the Love Center experience you've just given yourself:

♥ REMEMBER: It's not what you say or do that creates the Love Center. It's how you feel inside! Learning how to say "no" from the Love Center really helps your life works better!

✍ You may have felt the Love Center as you wrote that description, or you may have said the words to yourself without feeling the love. Either way helps you to see there is a choice. Write yourself a love note, and list any insights and growth you perceive in your awareness today:

♡ Give yourself a Love Center hug!

3

Make each demand specific with: who, what, when, and possibly where. See page 26 for tips on using your daily work pages.

Date: _____

I create the experience of	because my programming demands that	Cent. of Consc.	Path-way(s)

Link the Suffering With the Addictive Demand
Practice in Pinpointing

"... the key to using the Third Method is to look deeply within yourself to find the emotion-backed demand that you are using to upset yourself. It's this simple. Just become more consciously conscious of the cause-effect relationship between your addictions and the resulting unhappiness, and you will be on the escalator that can take you directly to the Fourth Center of Consciousness." **Handbook to Higher Consciousness,** Chapter 13.

♥ In order to effectively link whatever unhappiness you are experiencing with an addictive demand, you need to know precisely what it is you're demanding. To help you do this, think of a repeating pattern in your life that you keep getting upset over.

✍ Briefly note the pattern:

♥ Put yourself back into the most recent situation as if it were happening right now. Answer briefly to yourself any of the following questions that seem to apply: What separating emotions am I feeling? What pain or tensions are in my body? What do my posture and face look like? What am I telling myself? Exactly what am I resisting in this situation? Or about myself? What threat does this person or situation represent to me? What is the worst that could happen? What is it about me that I think people can't love? What change am I demanding in order to feel happy and enough? Of myself? Of others?

✍ Write down any awarenesses or insights you gained of programming that was not previously apparent to you:

✍ Write down your addictive demand as clearly and precisely as you can pinpoint it:

I create the experience of_____

because my programming demands that _____

_____

_____

♥ This form reminds you that it is only the addictive programming in your mind that's causing your emotional experience, not the situation. Sometimes using the form is enough for you to uplevel an addictive demand to a preference. Sometimes further work is needed. Tomorrow, you can use another method on this demand to give you practice in reprogramming.

✍ Now write yourself a loving statement:

♡ And give yourself an encouraging hug!

4

Date: _____

I create the experience of	because my programming demands that	Cent. of Consc.	Path-way(s)

Consciousness Focusing
Formulating Reprogramming Phrases

"Choose a reprogramming phrase that is short, pithy, and that feels good . . . that directly refers to the situation . . . ." **Handbook to Higher Consciousness,** Chapter 14.

✍ Rewrite the demand you worked with yesterday, or choose one from today that you're ready to work with because you linked your suffering to the addiction, and you *know* it's not only the situation that's causing you to feel upset:

I create the experience of _____

because my programming demands that_____

_____

♥ One of the best guidelines for forming a reprogramming phrase is to make a statement you want to live with and that you can imagine experiencing. Pick a beginning that feels possible and good. Here are some choices:

Beginning a Reprogramming Phrase	
I love . . .	I can choose to see myself as . . .
I can feel . . .	I have the right to . . .
I'm okay . . .	I can learn to accept . . .
I'm learning to love . . .	I'm willing to . . .

✍ Write several possible reprogramming phrases related to the demand:

★ Put a star by the phrase that you most strongly respond to with "Yes! That's what I want to tell myself!"

♥ Focus on the phrase. Close your eyes and breathe deeply. Let yourself relax and feel peaceful. As you begin to relax, repeat your phrase slowly and meditatively for several minutes.

✍ Remember, you can take that phrase with you into any situation where that or similar demands are triggered. Describe your experience of using the phrase:

✍ Write yourself a love note that reminds you of a way you are growing:

♡ Give yourself a hug!

5

Make each demand specific with: who, what, when, and possibly where. See page 26 for tips on using your daily work pages.

Date: _____

I create the experience of	because my programming demands that	Cent. of Consc.	Path-way(s)

Instant Consciousness Doubler
With Another Person

"The Instant Consciousness Doubler helps us realize that there are no 'others' in this world." **Handbook to Higher Consciousness, Chapter 16.**

♥ Think of a situation today in which your friend, relationship partner, or business associate really "got on your nerves." (If you can't think of a time today, scan back over the past week.)

✍ Briefly, describe what that person *actually* said or did. Avoid judgments or mind reading about his or her intentions:

✍ Recall a time you said or did or thought something similar. Write about that on the next page. If you can't think of such a time, imagine doing or thinking something similar:

✍ Get in touch with the place in you that feels loving and accepting toward yourself. Realize that the words, actions, or thoughts you used in the similar situation were based on your programming. Now, expand that love and acceptance to include the person you recently felt separate from. Write how it feels:

✍ Take a deep breath. Imagine that you are the other person with his/her programming. Put yourself in his/her shoes. Let yourself experience how you would have said or done exactly the same thing if you had his/her programming. Feel compassion for all of us acting like robots of our programming until we see that we have a choice. To increase your understanding, write what you might feel if you were in that other person's shoes:

✍ Write yourself a loving note. Write how you perceive yourself growing today:

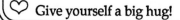

♡ Give yourself a big hug!

6

Make each demand specific with: who, what, when, and possibly where. See page 26 for tips on using your daily work pages.

Date: _____

I create the experience of	because my programming demands that	Cent. of Consc.	Path-way(s)

Handling Your Addictions
Getting Specific With Your Demands

"Be very specific in pinpointing the demand. Exactly what do you want in that situation? What would you like to change in that situation? Tune in to your feelings and check to make sure you feel that you've pinpointed the demand which is causing your suffering." **Handbook to Higher Consciousness,** Chapter 14.

♥ Remember, what you've been doing each day is handling your addictions. "Handling" means three things: 1) pinpointing your specific demand, 2) taking intellectual responsibility (without blaming yourself), and 3) using a method.

★ To make sure you are pinpointing your demands as specifically as you can, put a star by one above, and write the answers to these questions:

✍ *Who* is the demand on?

✍ Exactly *what* are you demanding?

✍ *When* was it triggered?

✍ *Where* did the demand get triggered?

♥ Every time you pinpoint a demand, be sure you know what its "4 W's" are, even if the "when" and "where" are not written as part of the demand.

✍ Take intellectual responsibility without blaming yourself or anyone else. Write one sentence; e.g., "It's my addictive programming that creates this unhappiness, not the situation," or "I take responsibility for creating this suffering":

✍ Now use a method. Describe the same situation from the Conscious-Awareness Center. Write about yourself in the third person, nonjudgmentally observing what's happening inside and outside of you:

✍ You are lovable with every experience that your programming creates. Write a reminder to love yourself and to acknowledge the ways you've been growing:

♡ Remember that hug!

7

Make each demand specific with: who, what, when, and possibly where. See page 26 for tips on using your daily work pages.

Date: _____

I create the experience of	because my programming demands that	Cent. of Consc.	Path-way(s)

The Twelve Pathways
Being Here Now—Pathways 4, 5, and 6

"The world thus tends to be your mirror. A peaceful person lives in a peaceful world. An angry person creates an angry world. A helpful person generates helpful, loving energy in others." **Handbook to Higher Consciousness,** Chapter 6.

4. I always remember that I have everything I need to enjoy my here and now—unless I am letting my consciousness be dominated by demands and expectations based on the dead past or the imagined future.

5. I take full responsibility here and now for everything I experience, for it is my own programming that creates my actions and also influences the reactions of people around me.

6. I accept myself completely here and now and consciously experience everything I feel, think, say, and do (including my emotion-backed addictions) as a necessary part of my growth into higher consciousness.

♥ Think of a time during your day when you were not experiencing being "here and now" or when you judged or criticized yourself.

✍ Write a brief description of how you felt:

♥ Say the Fourth, Fifth, and Sixth Pathways as you replay the incident in your mind. You may wish to say them more than once.

✍ Write what you experienced as you mentally replayed the incident while saying Pathways 4, 5, and 6:

✍ Write yourself a loving note and acknowledge the beauty that is in you right now:

♡ Give yourself a great BIG hug!

8

Make each demand specific with: who, what, when, and possibly where. See page 26 for tips on using your daily work pages.

Date: _____

I create the experience of	because my programming demands that	Cent. of Consc.	Path-way(s)

Centers of Consciousness
Imagining ... the Fifth Center

"... you will begin to feel that you live in a friendly world that will always give you 'enough' when you live in the higher Centers of Consciousness. ... your world is perfect from the point of view of continually providing you with precisely the life experiences that you need for your overall development as a conscious being." Handbook to Higher Consciousness, Chapter 11.

★ Put a star by a demand above in which you felt particularly caught in the Security, Sensation, or Power Center of Consciousness.

♥ Imagine that situation is happening right now. Use your imagination to experience the Fifth Center—*Cornucopia*. This center emphasizes the gentleness or intensity of the lesson, appreciation that you created the lesson with the particular people involved, and/or welcoming the lesson and the opportunity for growth.

✍ Write how you could experience the situation as a lesson which is part of the abundance of your life:

✍ Now, imagine that you are in the same situation as it happened. Instead of creating separating emotions, you create joy, wonder, and a feeling of having more than you need to be happy. Write how you could experience that situation by appreciating the "cornucopia" life is offering you:

✍ Be gentle with yourself! If you can *see* the "strawberries" (the things in your life to appreciate) yet not *feel* appreciation, that's okay. Enjoy yourself with whatever you feel. Write yourself a note about the strawberries of being you:

♡ Feel the pleasure of loving yourself and put it into a hug!

9

Make each demand specific with: who, what, when, and possibly where. See page 26 for tips on using your daily work pages.

Date: _____

I create the experience of	because my programming demands that	Cent. of Consc.	Path-way(s)

Link the Suffering With the Addictive Demand
Exploring Ripoffs

"You make a giant step toward higher consciousness when you become fully aware of the price in happiness you must pay for each addiction." **Handbook to Higher Consciousness,** Chapter 4.

♥ In order to make the connection that it is your addictive demand that's basically causing your unhappiness (not you, other people, or events), you must first be aware of how your programming is penalizing you—like a hidden dagger inside you!

★ Choose a demand from above and put a star by it.

♥ Turn to page 227 listing ripoffs. Examine the many areas and ways in which demands diminish your happiness.

✍ In the following list, circle the ways this addiction is hurting you. Add words to make the list specific to your addiction; e.g., *where* is your body tense? From *whom* are you feeling separate?

110

1. Body reactions: tension, constricted breath, rapid heartbeat...

2. Emotions: fear, frustration, anger...

3. Attitude toward self: low self-esteem...

4. Attitude toward others: judgmental, inability to feel close...

5. Energy, time: low, lost, wasted...

6. Perception of what is happening in life: distorted, illusory, inability to see surrounding beauty...

7. Spontaneity, creativity, openness: compulsive, inflexible, blocked...

8. Humor: no humor, serious problem, worried face...

9. Cooperative relationships with other people: triggering others' addictions...

10. Alternatives and choices: limited perspective, "tunnel vision"...

11. Making changes: limited ability due to wasted energy and lack of insight...

12. Enjoying your life: not enough, protecting and defending...

♥ All of these ripoffs are basically caused by your demand. Avoid blaming your upset feelings on someone else, a situation, or what you said or did. *Blame your programming—NOT YOU!* Sometimes, becoming aware of how that demand makes you upset is all that you need to be willing to uplevel the demand to a preference. At other times, you may choose to hold on to the addictive demand. You can love yourself either way!

✎ Now write yourself a loving note and remind yourself of the growing awareness you experienced today:

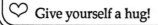

♡ Give yourself a hug!

10

Make each demand specific with: who, what, when, and possibly where. See page 26 for tips on using your daily work pages.

Date: _____

I create the experience of	because my programming demands that	Cent. of Consc.	Path-way(s)

Consciousness Focusing
Using a Phrase with Energy

"When you see clearly that it is your addiction that is immediately causing your suffering and not the situation in itself, and when you see how unnecessary it is to make the demands you have been making, then you are ready to start reprogramming." **Handbook to Higher Consciousness,** Chapter 14.

♥ Use Consciousness Focusing when you want inner peace, love, and freedom from your addictive programming *more* than you want what you are demanding.

★ Put a star by an addictive demand above that you feel you are ready to uplevel to a preference. (If you're not ready to uplevel any of today's demands, pick one you can imagine wanting to uplevel.)

✍ Sometimes it takes formulating several phrases before you find one that feels right. Come up with ones that feel good and that energize you. Using the seven guidelines on page 21, write at least five reprogramming phrases related to the demand you chose:

★ Put a star by the reprogramming phrase that feels best to you.

♥ Visualize the incident in which you triggered the demand. Realize that with motivation to get free of the addictive programming, you can have inner peace instead of emotional turmoil. With added intensity, say one of your reprogramming phrases silently or aloud, over and over for several minutes.

✍ Write how it felt to use that phrase:

♥ Use this phrase tomorrow while you are walking, jogging, or doing any kind of physical activity.

✍ Write yourself a loving reprogramming phrase below, and say it softly to yourself several times right now:

♥ I am ♥
lovable...

♡ Give yourself a tender hug.

113

11

Make each demand specific with: who, what, when, and possibly where. See page 26 for tips on using your daily work pages.

Date: _____

I create the experience of	because my programming demands that	Cent. of Consc.	Path- way(s)

Addictive and Preferential Programming

"Every addiction leaves us vulnerable; preferences enable us to continually enjoy life. When our biocomputers operate from preferential programming, our happiness is not affected—regardless of whether the outside world fits our preferences or not." **Handbook to Higher Consciousness**, Appendix 1.

♥ We can more or less enjoy our day when things go the way we want. When things don't go the way we want, our internal experience depends on whether our programmed response is addictive or preferential.

♥ Scan your day for situations you reacted to with addictive programming. You know an addiction has been triggered if 1) you feel separating emotions, 2) you feel body tension, 3) your rational mind keeps churning over the same thing, or 4) your life seems bogged down by a problem. You can use the above addictive demands to help you with this perspective of your day.

✍ Outline these situations in six words or less, such as "My car wouldn't start":

♥ Now shift into an awareness of the times today when you reacted with preferential programming to situations you didn't like. These incidents can be less obvious than the ones you get upset about since our minds don't snag on them. Yet noticing how much preferential programming we already have can be refreshing feedback. Realizing how much you're already winning can inspire you to keep on winning! Recall from your day the moments when you felt emotionally peaceful, your body felt relaxed, and your mind did not get stuck on a tape loop— even when things did not go as you would have liked.

✍ List those times here:

✍ Write yourself a gentle note and remind yourself that you are beautiful, capable, and lovable just the way you are:

♡ Hug yourself with compassion for both your addictive and preferential programming.

115

12

Make each demand specific with: who, what, when, and possibly where. See page 26 for tips on using your daily work pages.

Date: _____

I create the experience of	because my programming demands that	Cent. of Consc.	Path-way(s)

Combining Methods
Pathways; Centers of Consciousness

"Because you have created a beautiful, peaceful world in which you now live, you are helping everyone around you find the beautiful, peaceful place inside. And you can accept help without feeling that an obligation is created." **Handbook to Higher Consciousness,** Chapter 11.

✍ Which pathways that you chose above had the most meaning for you? Write down particular insights you got from saying them:

✍ On the next page, write a brief description of an incident today in which you created separating emotions:

116

✍Now rewrite the scene, imagining that you experience it from the Love Center:

✍ Rewrite the scene again, this time with the sense of abundance and opportunity for growth that comes from the Cornucopia Center:

✍ Write down the "wins" you had today in your consciousness growth:

♡ Hug yourself!

13

Make each demand specific with: who, what, when, and possibly where. See page 26 for tips on using your daily work pages.

Date: _____

I create the experience of	because my programming demands that	Cent. of Consc.	Path-way(s)

The Twelve Pathways
Interacting With Others—Pathways 7, 8, and 9

"Everyone and everything around you is your teacher." **Handbook to Higher Consciousness**, Chapter 5.

7. I open myself genuinely to all people by being willing to fully communicate my deepest feelings, since hiding in any degree keeps me stuck in my illusion of separateness from other people.

8. I feel with loving compassion the problems of others without getting caught up emotionally in their predicaments that are offering them messages they need for their growth.

9. I act freely when I am tuned in, centered, and loving, but if possible I avoid acting when I am emotionally upset and depriving myself of the wisdom that flows from love and expanded consciousness.

★ Put a star by a demand above that was on someone else. Say that demand, then the Seventh Pathway, the same demand again, then the Eighth Pathway, the demand once again, and then the Ninth Pathway.

✍ Write what you experienced as you alternated the demand with those three pathways:

✍ Write how you might have felt or acted differently if the insights reflected in Pathways 7, 8, and 9 had been in your consciousness at the time the demand was triggered:

✍ Enjoy the journey! Write yourself an encouraging note about the "wins" you've had today in your consciousness growth:

♡ Give yourself a reassuring hug!

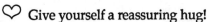

14

Make each demand specific with: who, what, when, and possibly where. See page 26 for tips on using your daily work pages.

Date: _____

I create the experience of	because my programming demands that	Cent. of Consc.	Path-way(s)

Centers of Consciousness
Watching From the Sixth Center

"It is liberating to have a Center from which your Conscious-awareness watches your body and mind perform on the lower five centers." **Handbook to Higher Consciousness, Chapter 9.**

✍ Stop the movie of your day by focusing on one incident in which you triggered separating emotions. Give a two- or three-sentence description of what happened in that scene:

♥ Take a deep breath. Now, mentally step back from the situation and create the drama using the Conscious-Awareness Center. You are now an impartial observer, watching and not identifying with the character (using "she" or "he" instead of "I") in the drama. Witness the scene moment by moment without judging, analyzing, generalizing, or labeling what is happening.

✍ Write a description of the scene using the Sixth Center. Remember: NO JUDGMENTS!

✍ You're doing fine! Appreciate yourself for continuing to use the workbook. Write any insights you got today:

♡ And give yourself a great big loving hug!

15

Make each demand specific with: who, what, when, and possibly where. See page 26 for tips on using your daily work pages.

Date: _____

I create the experience of	because my programming demands that	Cent. of Consc.	Path-way(s)

Link the Suffering With the Addictive Demand
Exploring Payoffs

"Changes leading to happiness come most rapidly when you can fully engage both your ego and rational mind (two of your most powerful faculties) in the game of helping you eliminate each addiction." **Handbook to Higher Consciousness, Chapter 13.**

♥ Each time you hold on to an addiction, there is a real or imaginary "payoff" you think you'll get. Identifying and questioning the value of these payoffs will help you to be aware of why your programming is hanging on to that demand.

★ Put a star by a demand pinpointed above.

✍ Using the list that follows as a general guide, check the payoffs you think you get by holding on to your demands and those emotions. Add specific details; e.g., who will give you attention, which other addictions you get to avoid confronting:

❑ Get to be right, feel superior.

❑ Get attention, sympathy, comfort, agreement, camaraderie.

❑ Avoid taking responsibility for how I feel. I can blame_____

❑ Get to avoid confronting other addictions. _____

❑ People won't think I'm_____

❑ Excuse for poor performance; people won't reject me.

❑ People will know I'm a good_____

❑ Feels safe and familiar.

❑ Feels safe to keep a distance from_____

❑ Get to play martyr and/or the victim role.

❑ Get to enjoy the fantasy.

❑ Get to feel close to others who have the same addictions._____

❑ Feel a sense of intensity and aliveness.

❑ I/he/she will change._____

❑ They'll make it up to me._____

★ Which one do you feel is the strongest? Put a star by that payoff.

✍ Focusing on that payoff, check any insights you have about the
supposed payoff that makes you hold on to your addiction:

❑ It's an illusion; I don't really get that payoff.

❑ "What is" doesn't change by holding on to the addiction.

❑ When I get this payoff it lasts only temporarily and doesn't bring
continued peace and happiness.

❑ It's not enough.

❑ Getting this payoff doesn't feel as good as love.

❑ I create more separateness in my life.

❑ I lose out on the fullness of what is available in my life. I cut down on my
involvement.

❑ I solidify my judgmental opinions by holding on.

❑ I'm setting up my next lesson.

❑ I can put energy into getting or enjoying that "payoff" from a preferential
space.

❑ I can go for that payoff directly; e.g., ask for attention, choose to change
something in my life.

❑ Other insights:

✍ Be patient with yourself. You are growing in awareness.
Write yourself some loving thoughts in a note:

♡ Give yourself a warm hug.

16

Make each demand specific with: who, what, when, and possibly where. See page 26 for tips on using your daily work pages.

Date: _____

I create the experience of	because my programming demands that	Cent. of Consc.	Path-way(s)

Consciousness Focusing
Intensive Mode

"But it's your determination and will to be free of the addiction that really accomplishes the reprogramming...." **Handbook to Higher Consciousness,** Chapter 14.

♥ Using the Intensive Mode of Consciousness Focusing may bring about a fast and dramatic shift in your programming.

★ Put a star by an addictive demand above in which intense heavy emotions are involved, about which you have become keenly aware of its ripoffs, *and* that you feel you're ready to uplevel to a preference. (If none of the demands above fit that description, find a previous days' demand and rewrite it.)

✍ Write several reprogramming phrases, using the seven guide-lines on page 21."

★ Put a star by the one that makes the strongest impact on your positive energies.

♥ Find a place where you can be by yourself to focus on the phrase. Review the ripoffs of the demand. Keeping them in mind, build up a strong determination to be free of the old programming. Start silently saying the phrase in your head, and tense your muscles. Allow intensity to build and let yourself experience whatever emotions come up. After you repeat the phrase as long as you want, keep your eyes closed and review the same situation, this time with your new phrase running silently in your head.

✍ Appreciate yourself for the freedom you are giving yourself. Write a note acknowledging ways you experienced an increase in your love today:

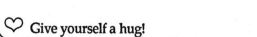

♡ Give yourself a hug!

17

Make each demand specific with: who, what, when, and possibly where. See page 26 for tips on using your daily work pages.

Date: _____

I create the experience of	because my programming demands that	Cent. of Consc.	Path-way(s)

Instant Consciousness Doubler
With Yourself

"We have at all times been lovable. A child may be naughty, but he is always lovable. And so we are all children as long as we are programmed with our lower consciousness addictions." **Handbook to Higher Consciousness,** Chapter 3.

✍ Focus on a time today when you felt something other than love or acceptance for yourself, when you told yourself you should have been different. Write what you felt and what you did that triggered the feeling:

✍ Take a deep breath. Write the name of someone you deeply love, respect, or admire:

♥ Imagine that he/she said or did what you said or did when you created that separation. Feel yourself loving and accepting him or her doing something similar.

✍ Write how that would feel. Perhaps you'd like to include what you might say to him or her with this loving feeling:

♥ Now, expand that love and compassion to include yourself. Give yourself the same understanding and acceptance that you give this other person. Remember that in your essence you are not your thoughts, actions, or programming.

✍ Write what you might tell yourself with the increased understanding and acceptance you deserve:

✍ Write yourself a loving, compassionate note:

♡ Give yourself some love with a BIG hug!

18

Make each demand specific with: who, what, when, and possibly where. See page 26 for tips on using your daily work pages.

Date: _____

I create the experience of	because my programming demands that	Cent. of Consc.	Path-way(s)

Combining Methods
Link the Suffering; Consciousness Focusing

"We learn to love others by accepting and loving ourselves—and vice versa." Handbook to Higher Consciousness, Chapter 8.

★ Choose the most persistent addictive demand above and put a star by it.

✍ List several ways that your demand penalizes you:

✍ Formulate several possible reprogramming phrases related to the demand. Write ones that feel good, that you would like to instill in your mind, and that you can imagine experiencing as a reality for you:

★ Choose the phrase that feels most energizing to you and put a star by it.

♥ Now, keeping in mind all the ways the addictive demand has ripped you off, repeat your reprogramming phrase over and over for several minutes with a determination to free yourself from the addiction.

✍ Take a deep breath and write yourself a note that's filled with joy and a sense of inner peace!

♡ And remember that hug!

19

Make each demand specific with: who, what, when, and possibly where. See page 26 for tips on using your daily work pages.

Date: _____

I create the experience of	because my programming demands that	Cent. of Consc.	Path-way(s)

The Twelve Pathways
Discovering My Conscious-Awareness—Pathways 10, 11, and 12

"We're just not that different from each other." **Handbook to Higher Consciousness**, Chapter 8.

10. I am continually calming the restless scanning of my rational mind in order to perceive the finer energies that enable me to unitively merge with everything around me.
11. I am constantly aware of which of the Seven Centers of Consciousness I am using, and I feel my energy, perceptiveness, love, and inner peace growing as I open all of the Centers of Consciousness.
12. I am perceiving everyone, including myself, as an awakening being who is here to claim his or her birthright to the higher consciousness planes of unconditional love and oneness.

✍ Think of a time today when your mind was striving for, clinging to, or rejecting something or someone. Briefly describe what you were telling yourself (continue writing on next page):

♥ Keeping that experience in mind, say Pathways 10, 11, and 12 slowly and meditatively. Do this several times.

✍ Write whatever happened inside you as you said those three pathways; e.g., insights, times when your mind wandered, calmness, resistance, new awareness:

♥ Say the Twelfth Pathway again as a reminder to accept yourself.

✍ Write yourself a note filled with love, and acknowledge the "wins" you had today in your consciousness growth:

♡ Give yourself a great big hug!

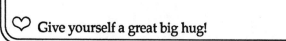

20

Make each demand specific with: who, what, when, and possibly where. See page 26 for tips on using your daily work pages.

Date: _____

I create the experience of	because my programming demands that	Cent. of Consc.	Path-way(s)

Centers of Consciousness
Playing Through the Various Centers

"One of the benefits of the seven-step consciousness scale is to enable you to see your drama from a perspective so that you can choose the filters you wish to use in generating your experience." **Handbook to Higher Consciousness,** Chapter 9.

✍ Write a brief, objective description of an incident in which you triggered separating emotions:

✍ Use your imagination to write a possible scenario of that same scene from each of the centers of consciousness below. Write which emotions you would feel; the thoughts that would be in your head; and, if you want, the possible actions that would come from those thoughts and emotions:

SECURITY:

SENSATION:

POWER:

LOVE:

CORNUCOPIA:

CONSCIOUS-AWARENESS:

✍ Notice any insights and shifts in perspective you got today, and give yourself some love in a note:

♡ Choose the Love or Cornucopia Center from which to hug yourself!

21

Make each demand specific with: who, what, when, and possibly where. See page 26 for tips on using your daily work pages.

Date: _____

I create the experience of	because my programming demands that	Cent. of Consc.	Path-way(s)

Link the Suffering With the Addictive Demand
Weighing Ripoffs and Payoffs

" 'Have I suffered enough?' " **Handbook to Higher Consciousness,** Chapter 13.

♥ When you first become aware of an addiction, you may not experience that you are suffering much. You also may feel that the payoffs for holding on are great. As you gain awareness of ripoffs and payoffs, you will begin to feel the real price you pay for holding on to your addiction and to realize that the reward in the payoffs is very scant.

★ Put a star by the heaviest addictive demand above.

♥ Turn to pages 227 and 228. Review the ripoffs and payoffs listed.

✍ Briefly list your ripoffs and payoffs on the next page. Use one to five words, such as "tension in neck," "frustration," and "I get to be right":

ACTUAL RIPOFFS   VS.   INTENDED PAYOFFS

✖ Put an "x" by each payoff you see as *illusory* (you don't actually get it by holding on to the demand) or *temporary* (you get temporary pleasure but it's not enough).

♥ Look at the balance of ripoffs and payoffs. Is the demand worth holding on to? Holding on to the demand—even with those payoffs—perpetuates isolation, crystallizes opinions, and prolongs suffering. You lose involvement, wisdom, and love.

✍ Write an acknowledgment of the beauty and perfection of your process of growth in a "mushy" love note to yourself:

♡ Hug yourself just for being you!

22

Make each demand specific with: who, what, when, and possibly where. See page 26 for tips on using your daily work pages.

Date: _____

I create the experience of	because my programming demands that	Cent. of Consc.	Path-way(s)

Consciousness Focusing
The Catalyst

"The Catalyst ALL WAYS US LIVING LOVE can be slowly and silently repeated to enable you to continuously tune in to that part of you that does not see others as him, her, or them—but always us." **Handbook to Higher Consciousness**, Chapter 13.

♥ You can use a general reprogramming phrase as a foreground figure against which your feelings, thoughts, and actions are the background. "All Ways Us Living Love" is a general phrase that we call the "Catalyst." You can use this phrase to help calm your mind when it's overloaded with addictive programming and thereby make room for understanding with your heart.

♥ Look over the demands you listed on the previous page. Recall the various situations today in which you felt emotionally triggered. Close your eyes and breathe deeply. Let yourself relax. Begin saying "All Ways Us Living Love," emphasizing a subsequent word each time. As you repeat the Catalyst slowly and meditatively for several minutes, allow your mind to reflect on those situations today, and imagine being back in them—this time feeling calm and peaceful.

✍ Describe your experience of using the Catalyst:

✍ Write down the "wins" you have recently had in your consciousness growth:

♡ Give yourself a great BIG hug!

23

Make each demand specific with: who, what, when, and possibly where. See page 26 for tips on using your daily work pages.

Date: _____

I create the experience of	because my programming demands that	Cent. of Consc.	Path-way(s)

The Law of Higher Consciousness

"Love everyone unconditionally—including yourself.
This law can enable you to find the hidden splendor within yourself and others." **Handbook to Higher Consciousness, Chapter 3.**

✍ List some of the times today when you could have applied the Law of Higher Consciousness, but didn't. Remember that the law includes appreciating and loving yourself unconditionally:

✍ Describe what those times might have been like if your programming had allowed you to love unconditionally:

✍ You are absolutely lovable just the way you are! Write yourself an encouraging note:

♡ And give yourself a loving, tender hug!

24

Make each demand specific with: who, what, when, and possibly where. See page 26 for tips on using your daily work pages.

Date: _____

I create the experience of	because my programming demands that	Cent. of Consc.	Path-way(s)

Combining Methods
Centers of Consciousness; Doubler; Catalyst

". . . you experience the power, the deep peace, and the exquisite beauty of letting your energy harmonize with the energies around you." **Handbook to Higher Consciousness**, Chapter 12.

★ Put a star by a demand you wrote above.

✍ Describe that incident from the Conscious-Awareness Center. Refer to yourself in the third person, nonjudgmentally witnessing your inner thoughts and feelings, and the outer actions of yourself and others:

✍ Now move into the Cornucopia Center. Describe the scene as it would be experienced with joy, gratitude, richness, and wonder:

✍ Now look at the person you felt separate from (yourself or someone else) through compassionate eyes. Understand that this person's behavior is a reflection of inner programming that may be trapping him or her in feeling upset. Realize that this person is doing his/her best to make his/her life work and to feel loved and loving. Write about this person from such a perspective:

✍ Keep the Catalyst, "All Ways Us Living Love," in the back of your mind as you write yourself a note. Give yourself credit for the ways you are opening yourself to more love in your life:

♡ Appreciate yourself with a hug!

25

Make each demand specific with: who, what, when, and possibly where. See page 26 for tips on using your daily work pages.

Date: _____

I create the experience of	because my programming demands that	Cent. of Consc.	Path-way(s)

The Twelve Pathways
All Twelve Pathways

"One interesting aspect of the Twelve Pathways is that if you can follow any one of them completely on the deeper levels, you will be using almost all of them." **Handbook to Higher Consciousness, Chapter 6.**

♥ Focus on the hardest time for you today. Recall the physical sensations and separating emotions you felt. Remember what thoughts went through your mind.

♥ As you stay focused on that time, say each of the Twelve Pathways with emphasis and expression.

✍ Write what changes happened in your **physical sensations:**

142

✍ Write what happened with your **emotional experience** as you said the pathways:

✍ Write what **insights** came to your mind:

✍ Write yourself a loving note and acknowledge how you see yourself growing today:

♡ Give yourself a BIG hug!

26

Date: _____

I create the experience of	because my programming demands that	Cent. of Consc.	Path-way(s)

Centers of Consciousness
Fourth, Fifth, and Sixth Centers

"A beautiful aspect of the consciousness scale is that each time you go up a step in the scale, your life gives you: 1. More energy. 2. More contact with people. 3. More enjoyment." Handbook to Higher Consciousness, Chapter 9.

★ Put a star by a demand above.

♥ Relax. Focus on the situation in which you created that demand, keeping in mind that the events stay the same. Imagine changing your emotional experience by using preferential programming. Re-create that scene in your mind and describe it:

✍ Through the **Love Center:**

✍ Through the **Cornucopia Center:**

✍ Through the **Conscious-Awareness Center:**

✍ Whatever is happening inside you is perfect for your enjoyment and/or your growth and openness to love. Write
what you appreciate in your life today—including what you
appreciate about yourself:

♡ Hug yourself!

27

Make each demand specific with: who, what, when, and possibly where. See page 26 for tips on using your daily work pages.

Date: _____

I create the experience of	because my programming demands that	Cent. of Consc.	Path-way(s)

Link the Suffering With the Addictive Demand
Comparing Ripoffs of a Demand With Benefits of a Preference

"In other words, with Preferential Programming, there is no way I can 'lose' and there is definitely a way that I can 'win.' " **Handbook to Higher Consciousness,** Chapter 23.

★ Put a star by a demand above that you would like to work with further.

✍ With this demand in mind, circle in the first column on the next page all the ways that this demand is keeping you from enjoying your life. Add any other details not listed:

✍ Now circle all the items in the second column that indicate the benefits you may receive when you successfully uplevel this demand to a preference. Add any other details that come to mind:

146

	Ripoffs of This Demand	Benefits of a Preference
Body	body tense, weak, constricted breath, rapid heartbeat,	body relaxed, breath normal, heartbeat normal,
Emotions	fear, frustration, anger,	acceptance, peace, love, happiness,
Attitude toward self	low self-esteem, limited feeling of love, judgmentalness,	high self-esteem, self-appreciation, emotional acceptance of self,
Attitude toward others	inability to feel close, limited love, criticalness,	emotional acceptance of others, closeness, love,

♥ Close your eyes and for a minute imagine what you will be doing and saying when this demand becomes a preference. Experience the differences between demanding and preferring.

✍ Write the ways you see yourself growing and opening up:

♡ Lovingly embrace yourself!

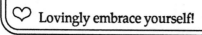

147

28

Make each demand specific with: who, what, when, and possibly where. See page 26 for tips on using your daily work pages.

Date: _____

I create the experience of	because my programming demands that	Cent. of Consc.	Path-way(s)

Consciousness Focusing
Reprogramming Phrases for Core Beliefs

"Your predictions and expectations are thus self-fulfilling. Since your consciousness creates your universe, all you have to do to change your world is to change your consciousness!" **Handbook to Higher Consciousness,** Chapter 6.

♥ We all base our experience of life on beliefs and assumptions, some of which are beneficial and some of which are self-destructive. We can change self-defeating core beliefs when we recognize them as programming rather than "reality" carved in stone or "just the way things are." One way to explore possible self-defeating core beliefs is to look for repeating patterns in the addictive demands we trigger day to day.

♥ Looking at the demands above, choose one, and explore what general attitudes might lie behind that demand. For example, if you create the experience of frustration and annoyance because your programming demands that you not eat a whole bag of tortilla chips at lunch today, perhaps you have a core belief that says "I can't be trusted to take care of myself," or maybe it's "I have

to be thin to be lovable." Examples of other core beliefs are "No matter how hard I try, it's never good enough," "Men (or women) will leave sooner or later," and "People don't want to listen to me."

🖋 Based on your demand, write out what some of your self-defeating thoughts or assumptions might be:

♥ You can come up with your own reprogramming phrases to challenge a self-destructive core belief and create a perception you'd like to experience; e.g., "Mother is doing the best she can and I can feel at peace with her," "I deserve to enjoy my life," or "I'm learning to feel beautiful, capable, and lovable."

🖋 Write out phrases that if used enough might free you from the possible self-defeating patterns you wrote above:

★ Select the phrase that feels best to you right now and put a star by it. Say the phrase 1,000 times tomorrow, using a counter as described on page 21.

🖋 Write a note reminding yourself of ways you are lovable:

♡ Show yourself some love with a hug!

149

29

Date: _____

I create the experience of	because my programming demands that	Cent. of Consc.	Path-way(s)

Instant Consciousness Doubler
With Another Person

"The love you have for yourself and the love you have for 'another' are building blocks joining together within you to create the beautiful edifice of real love." **Handbook to Higher Consciousness**, Chapter 3.

✍ Select a time today when you felt angry, afraid, resentful, or disgusted with someone else. Write what he or she did or said when you triggered those emotions:

✍ Increase your love and compassion for that person. Imagine what might have been his/her internal thoughts or feelings behind the words or actions today. Write them down:

♥ Remember that it's not that person's essential being that you felt separate from, but rather the things he or she was saying or doing—which was simply coming from programming. Your programming didn't like his/her programming!

✍ Write how this perspective can alter your experience of this person:

✍ Write a note to remind yourself of the beauty and perfection of you, just the way you are:

♡ Give yourself a great big hug!

30

The Highest Happiness

"You will increase your growth into higher consciousness by learning to flow energy into meeting the needs of 'others' as though they were your own needs." Handbook to Higher Consciousness, Chapter 11.

♥ As you increase your skill in handling security, sensation, and power center demands, you will discover a rise in energy, insight, appreciation for yourself and others, and happiness in your life. As you become richer and richer in happiness, you will find it increasingly satisfying to open your heart with more generosity. You can be more generous with your time to help others, with your emotional love and support, with the money that flows into your life, and with your possessions. Such inner richness will make you want to do more and more to help other people.

✍ In the space below, briefly write how you may choose to do something for someone (other than yourself) next week without any expectation that the person would "pay you back" or return your generosity in any way:

Suggestions to Spark Your Ideas

1. Buy a delicious snack and take it to a neighbor for no special reason.

2. Offer to help with something that you usually do not volunteer aid with.

3. Straighten up a room in your house in which you did not make the mess.

4. Show some extra love and caring for someone who seems upset, angry, or depressed.

5. Write a note of appreciation for someone you have felt separate from.

6. Volunteer your time with a worthy nonprofit organization such as Red Cross, Senior Citizen Center, or Women's Crisis Center.

7. Tithe 10% of your income to a civic or spiritual organization.

8. Take a few minutes to talk or play with a child with whom you usually don't spend time.

9. Go to the home of an elderly person and ask if you can help him/her for an hour in any way he/she could use it.

10. Carry a bag of canned food to a minister, priest, or rabbi and ask him/her to give it to a needy family.

11. Get some flowers and leave them by the front door of someone you don't know. Can you do it anonymously?

12. Write in some of your own ideas:

"...loving and serving yields the maximum of all the beautiful things that life can offer." Handbook to Higher Consciousness, Chapter 11.

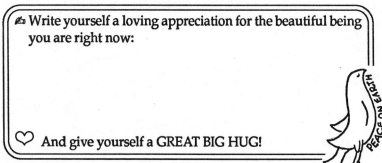

✍ Write yourself a loving appreciation for the beautiful being you are right now:

♡ And give yourself a GREAT BIG HUG!

Third
Month
of
Worksheets

1

Make each demand specific with: who, what, when, and possibly where. See page 26 for tips on using your daily work pages.

Date: _____

I create the experience of	because my programming demands that	Cent. of Consc.	Path-way(s)

The Twelve Pathways
Freeing Myself—Pathways 1, 2, and 3

"The Twelve Pathways to Higher Consciousness can show you how to accelerate your spiritual development and enable you to begin a new life of Living Love." **Handbook to Higher Consciousness, Chapter 4.**

1. I am freeing myself from security, sensation, and power addictions that make me try to forcefully control situations in my life and thus destroy my serenity and keep me from loving myself and others.
2. I am discovering how my consciousness-dominating addictions create my illusory version of the changing world of people and situations around me.
3. I welcome the opportunity (even if painful) that my minute-to-minute experience offers me to become aware of the addictions I must reprogram to be liberated from my robot-like emotional patterns.

★ For this practice, choose an addictive demand you wrote above and put a star by it.

♥ Keeping the demand in mind, open yourself to the inner wisdom you have for freeing yourself from addictive programming around that situation. To help you access that wisdom, say Pathways 1, 2, and 3 slowly and meditatively.

156

✍ Write down your insights and experience while you were saying the first three pathways:

✍ Write how any of these three pathways could have assisted you during any other part of your day today:

✍ Write three things you appreciate about yourself. They can be big or little appreciations. You are a lovable person!

1.

2.

3.

♡ Give yourself a supportive, encouraging hug!

2

Make each demand specific with: who, what, when, and possibly where. See page 26 for tips on using your daily work pages.

Date: _____

I create the experience of	because my programming demands that	Cent. of Consc.	Path-way(s)

Centers of Consciousness
The Love Center

"As you learn to live more and more in the Love Center of Consciousness, you will begin to find that you are creating a new world in which your consciousness resides. People and conditions are no longer a threat to you—for no one can threaten your preferences." **Handbook to Higher Consciousness,** Chapter 11.

★ Put a star by the demand above with which you experienced the strongest separating emotions.

♥ Now use your imagination! In your mind, go back to the situation you wrote the addictive demand about. Take a deep breath, relax, and imagine your *emotional experience* being different. See and feel yourself experiencing love, inner peace, happiness, compassion, and *emotional* acceptance of yourself, the situation, and the people around you. You may want to include alternatives you can see when you use this love filter.

Write a description of the Love Center experience you've just given yourself:

♥ REMEMBER: It's not what you say or do that creates the Love Center. It's how you feel inside! Learning how to say "no" from the Love Center really helps your life works better!

 You may have felt the Love Center as you wrote that description, or you may have said the words to yourself without feeling the love. Either way helps you to see there is a choice. Write yourself a love note, and list any insights and growth you perceive in your awareness today:

♡ Give yourself a Love Center hug!

3

Make each demand specific with: who, what, when, and possibly where. See page 26 for tips on using your daily work pages.

Date: _____

I create the experience of	because my programming demands that	Cent. of Consc.	Path-way(s)

Link the Suffering With the Addictive Demand
Practice in Pinpointing

"... the key to using the Third Method is to look deeply within yourself to find the emotion-backed demand that you are using to upset yourself. It's this simple. Just become more consciously conscious of the cause-effect relationship between your addictions and the resulting unhappiness, and you will be on the escalator that can take you directly to the Fourth Center of Consciousness." **Handbook to Higher Consciousness**, Chapter 13.

♥ In order to effectively link whatever unhappiness you are experiencing with an addictive demand, you need to know precisely what it is you're demanding. To help you do this, think of a repeating pattern in your life that you keep getting upset over.

✍ Briefly note the pattern:

160

♥ Put yourself back into the most recent situation as if it were happening right now. Answer briefly to yourself any of the following questions that seem to apply: What separating emotions am I feeling? What pain or tensions are in my body? What do my posture and face look like? What am I telling myself? Exactly what am I resisting in this situation? Or about myself? What threat does this person or situation represent to me? What is the worst that could happen? What is it about me that I think people can't love? What change am I demanding in order to feel happy and enough? Of myself? Of others?

✍ Write down any awarenesses or insights you gained of programming that was not previously apparent to you:

✍Write down your addictive demand as clearly and precisely as you can pinpoint it:

I create the experience of_____

because my programming demands that _____

_____

_____

♥ This form reminds you that it is only the addictive programming in your mind that's causing your emotional experience, not the situation. Sometimes using the form is enough for you to uplevel an addictive demand to a preference. Sometimes further work is needed. Tomorrow, you can use another method on this demand to give you practice in reprogramming.

✍ Now write yourself a loving statement:

♡ And give yourself an encouraging hug!

4

Make each demand specific with: who, what, when, and possibly where. See page 26 for tips on using your daily work pages.

Date: _____

I create the experience of	because my programming demands that	Cent. of Consc.	Path-way(s)

Consciousness Focusing
Formulating Reprogramming Phrases

"Choose a reprogramming phrase that is short, pithy, and that feels good . . . that directly refers to the situation . . . ." **Handbook to Higher Consciousness**, Chapter 14.

✍ Rewrite the demand you worked with yesterday, or choose one from today that you're ready to work with because you linked your suffering to the addiction, and you *know* it's not only the situation that's causing you to feel upset:

I create the experience of _____

because my programming demands that _____

_____

♥ One of the best guidelines for forming a reprogramming phrase is to make a statement you want to live with and that you can imagine experiencing. Pick a beginning that feels possible and good. Here are some choices:

162

✍ Write several possible reprogramming phrases related to the demand:

★ Put a star by the phrase that you most strongly respond to with "Yes! That's what I want to tell myself!"

♥ Focus on the phrase. Close your eyes and breathe deeply. Let yourself relax and feel peaceful. As you begin to relax, repeat your phrase slowly and meditatively for several minutes.

✍ Remember, you can take that phrase with you into any situation where that or similar demands are triggered. Describe your experience of using the phrase:

✍ Write yourself a love note that reminds you of a way you are growing:

♡ Give yourself a hug!

5

Make each demand specific with: who, what, when, and possibly where. See page 26 for tips on using your daily work pages.

Date: _____

I create the experience of	because my programming demands that	Cent. of Consc.	Path-way(s)

Instant Consciousness Doubler
With Another Person

"The Instant Consciousness Doubler helps us realize that there are no 'others' in this world." **Handbook to Higher Consciousness**, Chapter 16.

♥ Think of a situation today in which your friend, relationship partner, or business associate really "got on your nerves." (If you can't think of a time today, scan back over the past week.)

✍ Briefly, describe what that person *actually* said or did. Avoid judgments or mind reading about his or her intentions:

✍ Recall a time you said or did or thought something similar. Write about that on the next page. If you can't think of such a time, imagine doing or thinking something similar:

✍ Get in touch with the place in you that feels loving and accepting toward yourself. Realize that the words, actions, or thoughts you used in the similar situation were based on your programming. Now, expand that love and acceptance to include the person you recently felt separate from. Write how it feels:

✍ Take a deep breath. Imagine that you are the other person with his/her programming. Put yourself in his/her shoes. Let yourself experience how you would have said or done exactly the same thing if you had his/her programming. Feel compassion for all of us acting like robots of our programming until we see that we have a choice. To increase your understanding, write what you might feel if you were in that other person's shoes:

✍ Write yourself a loving note. Write how you perceive yourself growing today:

♡ Give yourself a big hug!

6

Make each demand specific with: who, what, when, and possibly where. See page 26 for tips on using your daily work pages.

Date: _____

I create the experience of	because my programming demands that	Cent. of Consc.	Path-way(s)

Handling Your Addictions
Getting Specific With Your Demands

"Be very specific in pinpointing the demand. Exactly what do you want in that situation? What would you like to change in that situation? Tune in to your feelings and check to make sure you feel that you've pinpointed the demand which is causing your suffering." **Handbook to Higher Consciousness,** Chapter 14.

♥ Remember, what you've been doing each day is handling your addictions. "Handling" means three things: 1) pinpointing your specific demand, 2) taking intellectual responsibility (without blaming yourself), and 3) using a method.

★ To make sure you are pinpointing your demands as specifically as you can, put a star by one above, and write the answers to these questions:

✍ *Who* is the demand on?

✍ Exactly *what* are you demanding?

✍ *When* was it triggered?

✍ *Where* did the demand get triggered?

♥ Every time you pinpoint a demand, be sure you know what its "4 W's" are, even if the "when" and "where" are not written as part of the demand.

✍ Take intellectual responsibility without blaming yourself or anyone else. Write one sentence; e.g., "It's my addictive programming that creates this unhappiness, not the situation," or "I take responsibility for creating this suffering":

✍ Now use a method. Describe the same situation from the Conscious-Awareness Center. Write about yourself in the third person, nonjudgmentally observing what's happening inside and outside of you:

✍ You are lovable with every experience that your programming creates. Write a reminder to love yourself and to acknowledge the ways you've been growing:

♡ Remember that hug!

7

Make each demand specific with: who, what, when, and possibly where. See page 26 for tips on using your daily work pages.

Date: _____

I create the experience of	because my programming demands that	Cent. of Consc.	Path-way(s)

The Twelve Pathways
Being Here Now—Pathways 4, 5, and 6

"The world thus tends to be your mirror. A peaceful person lives in a peaceful world. An angry person creates an angry world. A helpful person generates helpful, loving energy in others." **Handbook to Higher Consciousness,** Chapter 6.

4. I always remember that I have everything I need to enjoy my here and now—unless I am letting my consciousness be dominated by demands and expectations based on the dead past or the imagined future.
5. I take full responsibility here and now for everything I experience, for it is my own programming that creates my actions and also influences the reactions of people around me.
6. I accept myself completely here and now and consciously experience everything I feel, think, say, and do (including my emotion-backed addictions) as a necessary part of my growth into higher consciousness.

♥ Think of a time during your day when you were not experiencing being "here and now" or when you judged or criticized yourself.

✍ Write a brief description of how you felt:

♥ Say the Fourth, Fifth, and Sixth Pathways as you replay the incident in your mind. You may wish to say them more than once.

✍ Write what you experienced as you mentally replayed the incident while saying Pathways 4, 5, and 6:

✍ Write yourself a loving note and acknowledge the beauty that is in you right now:

♡ Give yourself a great BIG hug!

169

8

Make each demand specific with: who, what, when, and possibly where. See page 26 for tips on using your daily work pages.

Date: _____

I create the experience of	because my programming demands that	Cent. of Consc.	Path-way(s)

Centers of Consciousness
Imagining ... the Fifth Center

"... you will begin to feel that you live in a friendly world that will always give you 'enough' when you live in the higher Centers of Consciousness. ... your world is perfect from the point of view of continually providing you with precisely the life experiences that you need for your overall development as a conscious being." Handbook to Higher Consciousness, Chapter 11.

★ Put a star by a demand above in which you felt particularly caught in the Security, Sensation, or Power Center of Consciousness.

♥ Imagine that situation is happening right now. Use your imagination to experience the Fifth Center—*Cornucopia*. This center emphasizes the gentleness or intensity of the lesson, appreciation that you created the lesson with the particular people involved, and/or welcoming the lesson and the opportunity for growth.

✍ Write how you could experience the situation as a lesson which is part of the abundance of your life:

✍ Now, imagine that you are in the same situation as it happened. Instead of creating separating emotions, you create joy, wonder, and a feeling of having more than you need to be happy. Write how you could experience that situation by appreciating the "cornucopia" life is offering you:

✍ Be gentle with yourself! If you can *see* the "strawberries" (the things in your life to appreciate) yet not *feel* appreciation, that's okay. Enjoy yourself with whatever you feel. Write yourself a note about the strawberries of being you:

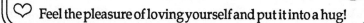

♡ Feel the pleasure of loving yourself and put it into a hug!

9

Make each demand specific with: who, what, when, and possibly where. See page 26 for tips on using your daily work pages.

Date: _____

I create the experience of	because my programming demands that	Cent. of Consc.	Path-way(s)

Link the Suffering With the Addictive Demand
Exploring Ripoffs

"You make a giant step toward higher consciousness when you become fully aware of the price in happiness you must pay for each addiction." **Handbook to Higher Consciousness, Chapter 4.**

♥ In order to make the connection that it is your addictive demand that's basically causing your unhappiness (not you, other people, or events), you must first be aware of how your programming is penalizing you—like a hidden dagger inside you!

★ Choose a demand from above and put a star by it.

♥ Turn to page 227 listing ripoffs. Examine the many areas and ways in which demands diminish your happiness.

🖎 In the following list, circle the ways this addiction is hurting you. Add words to make the list specific to your addiction; e.g., *where* is your body tense? From *whom* are you feeling separate?

172

1. Body reactions: tension, constricted breath, rapid heartbeat...

2. Emotions: fear, frustration, anger...

3. Attitude toward self: low self-esteem...

4. Attitude toward others: judgmental, inability to feel close...

5. Energy, time: low, lost, wasted...

6. Perception of what is happening in life: distorted, illusory, inability to see surrounding beauty...

7. Spontaneity, creativity, openness: compulsive, inflexible, blocked...

8. Humor: no humor, serious problem, worried face...

9. Cooperative relationships with other people: triggering others' addictions...

10. Alternatives and choices: limited perspective, "tunnel vision"...

11. Making changes: limited ability due to wasted energy and lack of insight...

12. Enjoying your life: not enough, protecting and defending...

♥ All of these ripoffs are basically caused by your demand. Avoid blaming your upset feelings on someone else, a situation, or what you said or did. *Blame your programming—NOT YOU!* Sometimes, becoming aware of how that demand makes you upset is all that you need to be willing to uplevel the demand to a preference. At other times, you may choose to hold on to the addictive demand. You can love yourself either way!

> ✍ Now write yourself a loving note and remind yourself of the growing awareness you experienced today:
>
> ♡ Give yourself a hug!

10

Make each demand specific with: who, what, when, and possibly where. See page 26 for tips on using your daily work pages.

Date: _____

I create the experience of	because my programming demands that	Cent. of Consc.	Path-way(s)

Consciousness Focusing
Using a Phrase with Energy

"When you see clearly that it is your addiction that is immediately causing your suffering and not the situation in itself, and when you see how unnecessary it is to make the demands you have been making, then you are ready to start reprogramming." Handbook to Higher Consciousness, Chapter 14.

♥ Use Consciousness Focusing when you want inner peace, love, and freedom from your addictive programming *more* than you want what you are demanding.

★ Put a star by an addictive demand above that you feel you are ready to uplevel to a preference. (If you're not ready to uplevel any of today's demands, pick one you can imagine wanting to uplevel.)

174

✍ Sometimes it takes formulating several phrases before you find one that feels right. Come up with ones that feel good and that energize you. Using the seven guidelines on page 21, write at least five reprogramming phrases related to the demand you chose:

★ Put a star by the reprogramming phrase that feels best to you.

♥ Visualize the incident in which you triggered the demand. Realize that with motivation to get free of the addictive programming, you can have inner peace instead of emotional turmoil. With added intensity, say one of your reprogramming phrases silently or aloud, over and over for several minutes.

✍ Write how it felt to use that phrase:

♥ Use this phrase tomorrow while you are walking, jogging, or doing any kind of physical activity.

✍ Write yourself a loving reprogramming phrase below, and say it softly to yourself several times right now:

♥ I am ♥
lovable...

♡ Give yourself a tender hug.

175

11

Make each demand specific with: who, what, when, and possibly where. See page 26 for tips on using your daily work pages.

Date: _____

I create the experience of	because my programming demands that	Cent. of Consc.	Path-way(s)

Addictive and Preferential Programming

"Every addiction leaves us vulnerable; preferences enable us to continually enjoy life. When our biocomputers operate from preferential programming, our happiness is not affected—regardless of whether the outside world fits our preferences or not." **Handbook to Higher Consciousness**, Appendix 1.

♥ We can more or less enjoy our day when things go the way we want. When things don't go the way we want, our internal experience depends on whether our programmed response is addictive or preferential.

♥ Scan your day for situations you reacted to with addictive programming. You know an addiction has been triggered if 1) you feel separating emotions, 2) you feel body tension, 3) your rational mind keeps churning over the same thing, or 4) your life seems bogged down by a problem. You can use the above addictive demands to help you with this perspective of your day.

✍ Outline these situations in six words or less, such as "My car wouldn't start":

♥ Now shift into an awareness of the times today when you reacted with preferential programming to situations you didn't like. These incidents can be less obvious than the ones you get upset about since our minds don't snag on them. Yet noticing how much preferential programming we already have can be refreshing feedback. Realizing how much you're already winning can inspire you to keep on winning! Recall from your day the moments when you felt emotionally peaceful, your body felt relaxed, and your mind did not get stuck on a tape loop— even when things did not go as you would have liked.

✍ List those times here:

✍ Write yourself a gentle note and remind yourself that you are beautiful, capable, and lovable just the way you are:

♡ Hug yourself with compassion for both your addictive and preferential programming.

12

Make each demand specific with: who, what, when, and possibly where. See page 26 for tips on using your daily work pages.

Date: _____

I create the experience of	because my programming demands that	Cent. of Consc.	Path-way(s)

Combining Methods
Pathways; Centers of Consciousness

"Because you have created a beautiful, peaceful world in which you now live, you are helping everyone around you find the beautiful, peaceful place inside. And you can accept help without feeling that an obligation is created." **Handbook to Higher Consciousness,** Chapter 11.

✍ Which pathways that you chose above had the most meaning for you? Write down particular insights you got from saying them:

✍ On the next page, write a brief description of an incident today in which you created separating emotions:

178

✍Now rewrite the scene, imagining that you experience it from the Love Center:

✍ Rewrite the scene again, this time with the sense of abundance and opportunity for growth that comes from the Cornucopia Center:

✍ Write down the "wins" you had today in your consciousness growth:

♡ Hug yourself!

13

Make each demand specific with: who, what, when, and possibly where. See page 26 for tips on using your daily work pages.

Date: _____

I create the experience of	because my programming demands that	Cent. of Consc.	Path-way(s)

The Twelve Pathways
Interacting With Others—Pathways 7, 8, and 9

"Everyone and everything around you is your teacher." **Handbook to Higher Consciousness,** Chapter 5.

7. I open myself genuinely to all people by being willing to fully communicate my deepest feelings, since hiding in any degree keeps me stuck in my illusion of separateness from other people.

8. I feel with loving compassion the problems of others without getting caught up emotionally in their predicaments that are offering them messages they need for their growth.

9. I act freely when I am tuned in, centered, and loving, but if possible I avoid acting when I am emotionally upset and depriving myself of the wisdom that flows from love and expanded consciousness.

★ Put a star by a demand above that was on someone else. Say that demand, then the Seventh Pathway, the same demand again, then the Eighth Pathway, the demand once again, and then the Ninth Pathway.

180

✍ Write what you experienced as you alternated the demand with those three pathways:

✍ Write how you might have felt or acted differently if the insights reflected in Pathways 7, 8, and 9 had been in your consciousness at the time the demand was triggered:

✍ Enjoy the journey! Write yourself an encouraging note about the "wins" you've had today in your consciousness growth:

♡ Give yourself a reassuring hug!

181

14

Make each demand specific with: who, what, when, and possibly where. See page 26 for tips on using your daily work pages.

Date: _____

I create the experience of	because my programming demands that	Cent. of Consc.	Path-way(s)

Centers of Consciousness
Watching From the Sixth Center

"It is liberating to have a Center from which your Conscious-awareness watches your body and mind perform on the lower five centers." **Handbook to Higher Consciousness,** Chapter 9.

✍ Stop the movie of your day by focusing on one incident in which you triggered separating emotions. Give a two- or three-sentence description of what happened in that scene:

♥ Take a deep breath. Now, mentally step back from the situation and create the drama using the Conscious-Awareness Center. You are now an impartial observer, watching and not identifying with the character (using "she" or "he" instead of "I") in the drama. Witness the scene moment by moment without judging, analyzing, generalizing, or labeling what is happening.

✍ Write a description of the scene using the Sixth Center. Remember: NO JUDGMENTS!

✍ You're doing fine! Appreciate yourself for continuing to use the workbook. Write any insights you got today:

♡ And give yourself a great big loving hug!

15

Make each demand specific with: who, what, when, and possibly where. See page 26 for tips on using your daily work pages.

Date: _____

I create the experience of	because my programming demands that	Cent. of Consc.	Path-way(s)

Link the Suffering With the Addictive Demand
Exploring Payoffs

"Changes leading to happiness come most rapidly when you can fully engage both your ego and rational mind (two of your most powerful faculties) in the game of helping you eliminate each addiction." **Handbook to Higher Consciousness, Chapter 13.**

♥ Each time you hold on to an addiction, there is a real or imaginary "payoff" you think you'll get. Identifying and questioning the value of these payoffs will help you to be aware of why your programming is hanging on to that demand.

★ Put a star by a demand pinpointed above.

✍ Using the list that follows as a general guide, check the payoffs you think you get by holding on to your demands and those emotions. Add specific details; e.g., who will give you attention, which other addictions you get to avoid confronting:

❑ Get to be right, feel superior.

❑ Get attention, sympathy, comfort, agreement, camaraderie.

❑ Avoid taking responsibility for how I feel. I can blame_____

❑ Get to avoid confronting other addictions. _____

❑ People won't think I'm_____

❑ Excuse for poor performance; people won't reject me.

❑ People will know I'm a good _____

❑ Feels safe and familiar.

❑ Feels safe to keep a distance from_____

❑ Get to play martyr and/or the victim role.

❑ Get to enjoy the fantasy.

❑ Get to feel close to others who have the same addictions._____

❑ Feel a sense of intensity and aliveness.

❑ I/he/she will change. _____

❑ They'll make it up to me. _____

★ Which one do you feel is the strongest? Put a star by that payoff.

✍ Focusing on that payoff, check any insights you have about the supposed payoff that makes you hold on to your addiction:

❑ It's an illusion; I don't really get that payoff.

❑ "What is" doesn't change by holding on to the addiction.

❑ When I get this payoff it lasts only temporarily and doesn't bring continued peace and happiness.

❑ It's not enough.

❑ Getting this payoff doesn't feel as good as love.

❑ I create more separateness in my life.

❑ I lose out on the fullness of what is available in my life. I cut down on my involvement.

❑ I solidify my judgmental opinions by holding on.

❑ I'm setting up my next lesson.

❑ I can put energy into getting or enjoying that "payoff" from a preferential space.

❑ I can go for that payoff directly; e.g., ask for attention, choose to change something in my life.

❑ Other insights:

✍ Be patient with yourself. You are growing in awareness. Write yourself some loving thoughts in a note:

♡ Give yourself a warm hug.

16

Make each demand specific with: who, what, when, and possibly where. See page 26 for tips on using your daily work pages.

Date: _____

I create the experience of	because my programming demands that	Cent. of Consc.	Path-way(s)

Consciousness Focusing
Intensive Mode

"But it's your determination and will to be free of the addiction that really accomplishes the reprogramming...." Handbook to Higher Consciousness, Chapter 14.

♥ Using the Intensive Mode of Consciousness Focusing may bring about a fast and dramatic shift in your programming.

★ Put a star by an addictive demand above in which intense heavy emotions are involved, about which you have become keenly aware of its ripoffs, *and* that you feel you're ready to uplevel to a preference. (If none of the demands above fit that description, find a previous days' demand and rewrite it.)

186

✍ Write several reprogramming phrases, using the seven guidelines on page 21."

★ Put a star by the one that makes the strongest impact on your positive energies.

♥ Find a place where you can be by yourself to focus on the phrase. Review the ripoffs of the demand. Keeping them in mind, build up a strong determination to be free of the old programming. Start silently saying the phrase in your head, and tense your muscles. Allow intensity to build and let yourself experience whatever emotions come up. After you repeat the phrase as long as you want, keep your eyes closed and review the same situation, this time with your new phrase running silently in your head.

✍ Appreciate yourself for the freedom you are giving yourself. Write a note acknowledging ways you experienced an increase in your love today:

♡ Give yourself a hug!

17

Make each demand specific with: who, what, when, and possibly where. See page 26 for tips on using your daily work pages.

Date: _____

I create the experience of	because my programming demands that	Cent. of Consc.	Path-way(s)

Instant Consciousness Doubler
With Yourself

"We have at all times been lovable. A child may be naughty, but he is always lovable. And so we are all children as long as we are programmed with our lower consciousness addictions." **Handbook to Higher Consciousness,** Chapter 3.

✎ Focus on a time today when you felt something other than love or acceptance for yourself, when you told yourself you should have been different. Write what you felt and what you did that triggered the feeling:

✍ Take a deep breath. Write the name of someone you deeply love, respect, or admire:

♥ Imagine that he/she said or did what you said or did when you created that separation. Feel yourself loving and accepting him or her doing something similar.

✍ Write how that would feel. Perhaps you'd like to include what you might say to him or her with this loving feeling:

♥ Now, expand that love and compassion to include yourself. Give yourself the same understanding and acceptance that you give this other person. Remember that in your essence you are not your thoughts, actions, or programming.

✍ Write what you might tell yourself with the increased understanding and acceptance you deserve:

✍ Write yourself a loving, compassionate note:

♡ Give yourself some love with a BIG hug!

18

Make each demand specific with: who, what, when, and possibly where. See page 26 for tips on using your daily work pages.

Date: _____

I create the experience of	because my programming demands that	Cent. of Consc.	Path-way(s)

Combining Methods
Link the Suffering; Consciousness Focusing

"We learn to love others by accepting and loving ourselves—and vice versa." **Handbook to Higher Consciousness,** Chapter 8.

★ Choose the most persistent addictive demand above and put a star by it.

✍ List several ways that your demand penalizes you:

✍ Formulate several possible reprogramming phrases related to the demand. Write ones that feel good, that you would like to instill in your mind, and that you can imagine experiencing as a reality for you:

★ Choose the phrase that feels most energizing to you and put a star by it.

♥ Now, keeping in mind all the ways the addictive demand has ripped you off, repeat your reprogramming phrase over and over for several minutes with a determination to free yourself from the addiction.

✍ Take a deep breath and write yourself a note that's filled with joy and a sense of inner peace!

♡ And remember that hug!

19

Make each demand specific with: who, what, when, and possibly where. See page 26 for tips on using your daily work pages.

Date: _____

I create the experience of	because my programming demands that	Cent. of Consc.	Path-way(s)

The Twelve Pathways
Discovering My Conscious-Awareness—Pathways 10, 11, and 12

"We're just not that different from each other." **Handbook to Higher Consciousness,** Chapter 8.

10. I am continually calming the restless scanning of my rational mind in order to perceive the finer energies that enable me to unitively merge with everything around me.

11. I am constantly aware of which of the Seven Centers of Consciousness I am using, and I feel my energy, perceptiveness, love, and inner peace growing as I open all of the Centers of Consciousness.

12. I am perceiving everyone, including myself, as an awakening being who is here to claim his or her birthright to the higher consciousness planes of unconditional love and oneness.

✍ Think of a time today when your mind was striving for, clinging to, or rejecting something or someone. Briefly describe what you were telling yourself (continue writing on next page):

♥ Keeping that experience in mind, say Pathways 10, 11, and 12 slowly and meditatively. Do this several times.

✍ Write whatever happened inside you as you said those three pathways; e.g., insights, times when your mind wandered, calmness, resistance, new awareness:

♥ Say the Twelfth Pathway again as a reminder to accept yourself.

✍ Write yourself a note filled with love, and acknowledge the "wins" you had today in your consciousness growth:

♡ Give yourself a great big hug!

20

Make each demand specific with: who, what, when, and possibly where. See page 26 for tips on using your daily work pages.

Date: _____

I create the experience of	because my programming demands that	Cent. of Consc.	Path-way(s)

Centers of Consciousness
Playing Through the Various Centers

"One of the benefits of the seven-step consciousness scale is to enable you to see your drama from a perspective so that you can choose the filters you wish to use in generating your experience." **Handbook to Higher Consciousness,** Chapter 9.

✍ Write a brief, objective description of an incident in which you triggered separating emotions:

✍ Use your imagination to write a possible scenario of that same scene from each of the centers of consciousness below. Write which emotions you would feel; the thoughts that would be in your head; and, if you want, the possible actions that would come from those thoughts and emotions:

SECURITY:

SENSATION:

POWER:

LOVE:

CORNUCOPIA:

CONSCIOUS-AWARENESS:

✍ Notice any insights and shifts in perspective you got today, and give yourself some love in a note:

♡ Choose the Love or Cornucopia Center from which to hug yourself!

195

21

Make each demand specific with: who, what, when, and possibly where. See page 26 for tips on using your daily work pages.

Date: _____

I create the experience of	because my programming demands that	Cent. of Consc.	Path-way(s)

Link the Suffering With the Addictive Demand
Weighing Ripoffs and Payoffs

" 'Have I suffered enough?' " **Handbook to Higher Consciousness,** Chapter 13.

♥ When you first become aware of an addiction, you may not experience that you are suffering much. You also may feel that the payoffs for holding on are great. As you gain awareness of ripoffs and payoffs, you will begin to feel the real price you pay for holding on to your addiction and to realize that the reward in the payoffs is very scant.

★ Put a star by the heaviest addictive demand above.

♥ Turn to pages 227 and 228. Review the ripoffs and payoffs listed.

🖎 Briefly list your ripoffs and payoffs on the next page. Use one to five words, such as "tension in neck," "frustration," and "I get to be right":

ACTUAL RIPOFFS   VS.   INTENDED PAYOFFS

_____   _____
_____   _____
_____   _____
_____   _____
_____   _____
_____   _____
_____   _____
_____   _____
_____   _____
_____   _____
_____   _____
_____   _____
_____   _____

✖ Put an "x" by each payoff you see as *illusory* (you don't actually get it by holding on to the demand) or *temporary* (you get temporary pleasure but it's not enough).

♥ Look at the balance of ripoffs and payoffs. Is the demand worth holding on to? Holding on to the demand—even with those payoffs—perpetuates isolation, crystallizes opinions, and prolongs suffering. You lose involvement, wisdom, and love.

> ✍ Write an acknowledgment of the beauty and perfection of your process of growth in a "mushy" love note to yourself:
>
> ♡ Hug yourself just for being you!

22

Make each demand specific with: who, what, when, and possibly where. See page 26 for tips on using your daily work pages.

Date: _____

I create the experience of	because my programming demands that	Cent. of Consc.	Path-way(s)

Consciousness Focusing
The Catalyst

"The Catalyst ALL WAYS US LIVING LOVE can be slowly and silently repeated to enable you to continuously tune in to that part of you that does not see others as him, her, or them—but always us." **Handbook to Higher Consciousness**, Chapter 13.

♥ You can use a general reprogramming phrase as a foreground figure against which your feelings, thoughts, and actions are the background. "All Ways Us Living Love" is a general phrase that we call the "Catalyst." You can use this phrase to help calm your mind when it's overloaded with addictive programming and thereby make room for understanding with your heart.

198

♥ Look over the demands you listed on the previous page. Recall the various situations today in which you felt emotionally triggered. Close your eyes and breathe deeply. Let yourself relax. Begin saying "All Ways Us Living Love," emphasizing a subsequent word each time. As you repeat the Catalyst slowly and meditatively for several minutes, allow your mind to reflect on those situations today, and imagine being back in them—this time feeling calm and peaceful.

✍ Describe your experience of using the Catalyst:

✍ Write down the "wins" you have recently had in your consciousness growth:

♡ Give yourself a great BIG hug!

23

Make each demand specific with: who, what, when, and possibly where. See page 26 for tips on using your daily work pages.

Date: _____

I create the experience of	because my programming demands that	Cent. of Consc.	Path-way(s)

The Law of Higher Consciousness

"Love everyone unconditionally—including yourself.
This law can enable you to find the hidden splendor within yourself and others." Handbook to Higher Consciousness, Chapter 3.

✍ List some of the times today when you could have applied the Law of Higher Consciousness, but didn't. Remember that the law includes appreciating and loving yourself unconditionally:

✍ Describe what those times might have been like if your programming had allowed you to love unconditionally:

✍ You are absolutely lovable just the way you are! Write yourself an encouraging note:

♡ And give yourself a loving, tender hug!

24

Make each demand specific with: who, what, when, and possibly where. See page 26 for tips on using your daily work pages.

Date: _____

I create the experience of	because my programming demands that	Cent. of Consc.	Path-way(s)

Combining Methods
Centers of Consciousness; Doubler; Catalyst

"... *you experience the power, the deep peace, and the exquisite beauty of letting your energy harmonize with the energies around you.*" **Handbook to Higher Consciousness,** Chapter 12.

★ Put a star by a demand you wrote above.

✍ Describe that incident from the Conscious-Awareness Center. Refer to yourself in the third person, nonjudgmentally witnessing your inner thoughts and feelings, and the outer actions of yourself and others:

✍ Now move into the Cornucopia Center. Describe the scene as it would be experienced with joy, gratitude, richness, and wonder:

✍ Now look at the person you felt separate from (yourself or someone else) through compassionate eyes. Understand that this person's behavior is a reflection of inner programming that may be trapping him or her in feeling upset. Realize that this person is doing his/her best to make his/her life work and to feel loved and loving. Write about this person from such a perspective:

✍ Keep the Catalyst, "All Ways Us Living Love," in the back of your mind as you write yourself a note. Give yourself credit for the ways you are opening yourself to more love in your life:

♡ Appreciate yourself with a hug!

25

Make each demand specific with: who, what, when, and possibly where. See page 26 for tips on using your daily work pages.

Date: _____

I create the experience of	because my programming demands that	Cent. of Consc.	Path-way(s)

The Twelve Pathways
All Twelve Pathways

"One interesting aspect of the Twelve Pathways is that if you can follow any one of them completely on the deeper levels, you will be using almost all of them." Handbook to Higher Consciousness, Chapter 6.

♥ Focus on the hardest time for you today. Recall the physical sensations and separating emotions you felt. Remember what thoughts went through your mind.

♥ As you stay focused on that time, say each of the Twelve Pathways with emphasis and expression.

✍ Write what changes happened in your **physical sensations:**

✍ Write what happened with your **emotional experience** as you said the pathways:

✍ Write what **insights** came to your mind:

✍ Write yourself a loving note and acknowledge how you see yourself growing today:

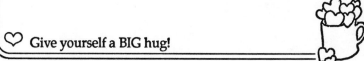

♡ Give yourself a BIG hug!

26

Make each demand specific with: who, what, when, and possibly where. See page 26 for tips on using your daily work pages.

Date: _____

I create the experience of	because my programming demands that	Cent. of Consc.	Path-way(s)

Centers of Consciousness
Fourth, Fifth, and Sixth Centers

"A beautiful aspect of the consciousness scale is that each time you go up a step in the scale, your life gives you: 1. More energy. 2. More contact with people. 3. More enjoyment." **Handbook to Higher Consciousness**, Chapter 9.

★ Put a star by a demand above.

♥ Relax. Focus on the situation in which you created that demand, keeping in mind that the events stay the same. Imagine changing your emotional experience by using preferential programming. Re-create that scene in your mind and describe it:

✍ Through the **Love Center:**

✍ Through the **Cornucopia Center:**

✍ Through the **Conscious-Awareness Center:**

> ✍ Whatever is happening inside you is perfect for your enjoy-
> ment and/or your growth and openness to love. Write
> what you appreciate in your life today—including what you
> appreciate about yourself:
>
>
>
>
> ♡ Hug yourself!

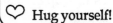

27

Date: _____

I create the experience of	because my programming demands that	Cent. of Consc.	Path-way(s)

Link the Suffering With the Addictive Demand
Comparing Ripoffs of a Demand With Benefits of a Preference

"In other words, with Preferential Programming, there is no way I can 'lose' and there is definitely a way that I can 'win.' " **Handbook to Higher Consciousness**, Chapter 23.

★ Put a star by a demand above that you would like to work with further.

✍ With this demand in mind, circle in the first column on the next page all the ways that this demand is keeping you from enjoying your life. Add any other details not listed:

✍ Now circle all the items in the second column that indicate the benefits you may receive when you successfully uplevel this demand to a preference. Add any other details that come to mind:

	Ripoffs of This Demand	Benefits of a Preference
Body	body tense, weak, constricted breath, rapid heartbeat,	body relaxed, breath normal, heartbeat normal,
Emotions	fear, frustration, anger,	acceptance, peace, love, happiness,
Attitude toward self	low self-esteem, limited feeling of love, judgmentalness,	high self-esteem, self-appreciation, emotional acceptance of self,
Attitude toward others	inability to feel close, limited love, criticalness,	emotional acceptance of others, closeness, love,

♥ Close your eyes and for a minute imagine what you will be doing and saying when this demand becomes a preference. Experience the differences between demanding and preferring.

✍ Write the ways you see yourself growing and opening up:

♡ Lovingly embrace yourself!

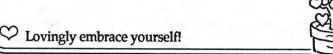

28

Make each demand specific with: who, what, when, and possibly where. See page 26 for tips on using your daily work pages.

Date: _____

I create the experience of	because my programming demands that	Cent. of Consc.	Path-way(s)

Consciousness Focusing
Reprogramming Phrases for Core Beliefs

"Your predictions and expectations are thus self-fulfilling. Since your consciousness creates your universe, all you have to do to change your world is to change your consciousness!" **Handbook to Higher Consciousness,** Chapter 6.

♥ We all base our experience of life on beliefs and assumptions, some of which are beneficial and some of which are self-destructive. We can change self-defeating core beliefs when we recognize them as programming rather than "reality" carved in stone or "just the way things are." One way to explore possible self-defeating core beliefs is to look for repeating patterns in the addictive demands we trigger day to day.

♥ Looking at the demands above, choose one, and explore what general attitudes might lie behind that demand. For example, if you create the experience of frustration and annoyance because your programming demands that you not eat a whole bag of tortilla chips at lunch today, perhaps you have a core belief that says "I can't be trusted to take care of myself," or maybe it's "I have

210

to be thin to be lovable." Examples of other core beliefs are "No matter how hard I try, it's never good enough," "Men (or women) will leave sooner or later," and "People don't want to listen to me."

✍ Based on your demand, write out what some of your self-defeating thoughts or assumptions might be:

♥ You can come up with your own reprogramming phrases to challenge a self-destructive core belief and create a perception you'd like to experience; e.g., "Mother is doing the best she can and I can feel at peace with her," "I deserve to enjoy my life," or "I'm learning to feel beautiful, capable, and lovable."

✍ Write out phrases that if used enough might free you from the possible self-defeating patterns you wrote above:

★ Select the phrase that feels best to you right now and put a star by it. Say the phrase 1,000 times tomorrow, using a counter as described on page 21.

✍ Write a note reminding yourself of ways you are lovable:

♡ Show yourself some love with a hug!

29

Date: _____

I create the experience of	because my programming demands that	Cent. of Consc.	Path-way(s)

Instant Consciousness Doubler
With Another Person

"The love you have for yourself and the love you have for 'another' are building blocks joining together within you to create the beautiful edifice of real love." Handbook to Higher Consciousness, Chapter 3.

✍ Select a time today when you felt angry, afraid, resentful, or disgusted with someone else. Write what he or she did or said when you triggered those emotions:

✍ Increase your love and compassion for that person. Imagine what might have been his/her internal thoughts or feelings behind the words or actions today. Write them down:

♥ Remember that it's not that person's essential being that you felt separate from, but rather the things he or she was saying or doing—which was simply coming from programming. Your programming didn't like his/her programming!

✍ Write how this perspective can alter your experience of this person:

✍ Write a note to remind yourself of the beauty and perfection of you, just the way you are:

♡ Give yourself a great big hug!

30

The Highest Happiness

"You will increase your growth into higher consciousness by learning to flow energy into meeting the needs of 'others' as though they were your own needs." Handbook to Higher Consciousness, Chapter 11.

♥ As you increase your skill in handling security, sensation, and power center demands, you will discover a rise in energy, insight, appreciation for yourself and others, and happiness in your life. As you become richer and richer in happiness, you will find it increasingly satisfying to open your heart with more generosity. You can be more generous with your time to help others, with your emotional love and support, with the money that flows into your life, and with your possessions. Such inner richness will make you want to do more and more to help other people.

✍ In the space below, briefly write how you may choose to do something for someone (other than yourself) next week without any expectation that the person would "pay you back" or return your generosity in any way:

Suggestions to Spark Your Ideas

1. Buy a delicious snack and take it to a neighbor for no special reason.

2. Offer to help with something that you usually do not volunteer aid with.

3. Straighten up a room in your house in which you did not make the mess.

4. Show some extra love and caring for someone who seems upset, angry, or depressed.

5. Write a note of appreciation for someone you have felt separate from.

6. Volunteer your time with a worthy nonprofit organization such as Red Cross, Senior Citizen Center, or Women's Crisis Center.

7. Tithe 10% of your income to a civic or spiritual organization.

8. Take a few minutes to talk or play with a child with whom you usually don't spend time.

9. Go to the home of an elderly person and ask if you can help him/her for an hour in any way he/she could use it.

10. Carry a bag of canned food to a minister, priest, or rabbi and ask him/her to give it to a needy family.

11. Get some flowers and leave them by the front door of someone you don't know. Can you do it anonymously?

12. Write in some of your own ideas:

"...loving and serving yields the maximum of all the beautiful things that life can offer." Handbook to Higher Consciousness, Chapter 11.

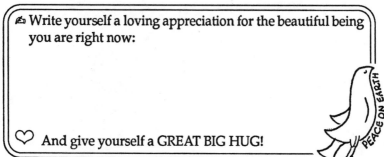

✍ Write yourself a loving appreciation for the beautiful being you are right now:

♡ And give yourself a GREAT BIG HUG!

PEACE ON EARTH

215

What's
Next?

Y ou may be wondering what to do for your next step in growth. Here are some ideas:

♥ From time to time, review this completed workbook and notice how you are growing. Use it to appreciate the addictive demands you've handled and the insights you've gained.

♥ Begin on another daily workbook. Keep on winning!

♥ Reread *Handbook to Higher Consciousness* and *Gathering Power Through Insight and Love*.

♥ Read *Discovering the Secrets of Happiness: My Intimate Story* to find inspiration in Ken's personal account of his lifelong journey of growth.

♥ Order some of the other publications listed on the following pages. Ken's *Conscious Person's Guide to Relationships* applies Living Love to relationships, and *How to Enjoy Your Life in Spite of It All* is a deeper explanation of the Twelve Pathways.

♥ Order some tapes. Get together with friends and listen to them. Ken's tapes explore questions people ask as they use the methods. The tapes focus on particular areas and how the methods apply.

♥ Get a pathways poster or one the pathways tapes to help you remember to say the pathways daily. Memorize them!

♥ Buy the four music cassettes with a range of feelings, words, and tunes that will help you remember you can choose to create love in your life in any moment.

♥ Be sure you are on our free mailing list so you will receive our catalog which tells you about trainings, publications, and news of Ken Keyes College.

♥ Consider attending or starting a Ken Keyes College Study Group. You can get information on study groups by calling the Registrar at (503) 267-6412.

♥ Attend a Living Love training at Ken Keyes College. These life-changing workshops have helped tens of thousands to create happier and happier lives. They range from a weekend to ten weeks. Some weekend trainings are available in larger cities throughout the nation. The following page gives further information on the workshops available through Ken Keyes College.

Ken Keyes College

You are invited to experience our loving seminars at the Ken Keyes College in Coos Bay, Oregon. Many people of diverse cultures, religions, and nationalities have found our gentle workshops profoundly helpful. They particularly appreciate the loving atmosphere, personal guidance, and hands-on experience in applying our practical techniques in their own lives. We also offer workshops in larger cities across the United States and Canada—all at nonprofit prices.

Some of our trainings are: Joy of Living, Increasing Your Self-Esteem, Healing Your Inner Child, Finding Inner Peace, and the ten-week comprehensive Body-Mind-Living Love course on the Science of Happiness. The emphasis in all of the trainings is to learn how to use practical methods to open your heart to appreciate and love yourself and others. Marriages have been saved and individuals have increased their happiness through these life-enriching workshops.

Our trainings at the College are held in an environment offering natural beauty and recreational opportunities. Across the street is a beautiful park with a delightful duck pond, tennis courts, and jogging trails. Nearby are beautiful beaches and forests. Located on scenic U.S. 101 on the Oregon coast, Coos Bay is easily accessible by car, bus, or air. Give yourself a gift you will cherish for a lifetime. Visit us soon.

You can write to the Registrar for training information: Ken Keyes College, 790 Commercial Avenue, Coos Bay, Oregon 97420, or telephone (503) 267-6412. Once on our mailing list, you will receive free information about new books, audio and video cassettes, posters, and workshops.

Ken Keyes College, Coos Bay, Oregon

Books by Ken

Handbook to Higher Consciousness
Ken Keyes, Jr., $6.95

This popular classic presents practical methods that can help you create happiness and unconditional love in your life. Countless people have experienced a dramatic change in their lives from the time they began applying the effective techniques explained in the *Handbook*. Some people, after reading this book, have bought out the bookstore and given copies to their friends. Over one million in print worldwide.

Discovering the Secrets of Happiness: My Intimate Story
Ken Keyes, Jr., $7.95

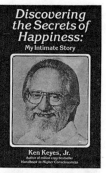

In this inspiring story, Ken shares his own journey of inner growth from an unfulfilled man seeking happiness through money and sex to a respected teacher of personal growth and world peace. Ken candidly expresses his successes and failures as he recounts how he gave up a lucrative business grossing $32 million dollars a year to dedicate his life to serving others, and how he has harnessed the power of "superlove" to create a deeply fulfilling marriage with his wife, Penny. He shows how you can enormously benefit from applying the secrets he discovered.

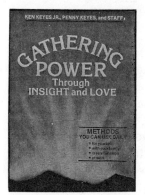

Gathering Power Through Insight and Love
Ken and Penny Keyes, $6.95

Here's how to do it! This outstanding book gives you detailed instructions on exactly how to develop the love inside you. It describes the 2-4-4 system for going from the separate-self to the unified-self: 2 Wisdom Principles, 4 Living Love Methods, and 4 Dynamic Processes. This book is based on their years of leading workshops. These skills are essential for those who want the most rapid rate of personal growth using the Science of Happiness.

A Conscious Person's Guide to Relationships
Ken Keyes, Jr., $5.95

If you're looking for effective new ways to give yourself a love-filled, satisfying, wonderful relationship, you will discover them in this book. Here finally is love without tears! This book contains seven guidelines for entering into a relationship, seven for bringing the power of unconditional love into your partnership, and seven for decreasing your involvement with gentleness. It describes sound principles that many people have found invaluable in creating a loving relationship. Over 250,000 in print.

Your Life Is a Gift
Ken Keyes, Jr., $5.95

Written in a lighthearted yet insightful fashion, here is a wonderful introduction to ways you can create your own happiness. This charming book, geared toward those embarking on personal growth, shows how simple it is to experience life with joy and purpose by insightfully guiding your thoughts and actions. Many people feel as though it had been written just for them. Filled with amusing and endearing drawings, this is a treasured gift book for all ages. 175,000 in print.

How to Enjoy Your Life in Spite of It All
Ken Keyes, Jr., $5.95

Learn to enjoy your life no matter what others say or do! The Twelve Pathways explained in this book are a modern, practical condensation of thousands of years of accumulated wisdom. Using these proven pathways will help you change your thoughts from separating, automatic reactions to practical, loving ways of thinking. They promote deep levels of insight, and help bring increased energy, inner peace, love, and perceptiveness into your moment-to-moment living. A must for people who are interested in their personal growth. 90,000 in print.

Prescriptions for Happiness
Ken Keyes, Jr., $4.95

Use these easy-to-remember secrets for happiness. Works for both children and adults. Designed for busy people, this book can be absorbed in about an hour. These simple prescriptions work wonders. They help you put more fun and aliveness into your interactions with people. Learn to ask for what you want with love in your heart. Benefit from techniques that boost insight, love, and enjoyment in our uncertain world. 144,000 in print.

Taming Your Mind
Ken Keyes, Jr., $7.95

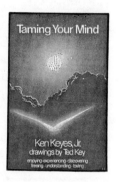

This enjoyable classic (which has been in print for almost 40 years) shows you how to transform your rational mind into a useful servant. These important "Tools for Thinking" can enormously improve your success in making sound decisions, getting along with people, being more effective in business—and working with others to build a better world. Written in an entertaining style with drawings by world famous cartoonist Ted Key, it was adopted by two national book clubs. Over 100,000 copies in print.

Your Heart's Desire—
A Loving Relationship
Ken Keyes, Jr., $4.95

Do you want to bring the magic of enduring love into your relationship? All of us have had a taste of what heart-to-heart love is like. We cherish those times and strive to experience them continuously. Using your rich inner resources, this book can inspire you to create a more loving relationship—without your partner having to change! It can help you to beautifully deepen the harmony, love, empathy, and trust in your relationship.

The Hundredth Monkey
Ken Keyes, Jr., Pocketbook, $2.00

There is no cure for nuclear war—ONLY PRE-VENTION! This book shows you that we have the creativity and power to change both ourselves and the world. You'll find here the facts about our nuclear predicament that some people don't want you to know. Internationally acclaimed—over one million copies have been distributed throughout the world. This dynamic little book has been translated into nine languages, including Russian.

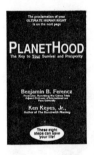

PlanetHood
Benjamin B. Ferencz and
Ken Keyes, Jr., Pocketbook, $2.50

This breakthrough book, which is the sequel to *The Hundredth Monkey*, explains how you can personally give yourself and your family a future in this nuclear age. It tells how we can replace the *law of force* with the *force of law*. It explains eight ways you can personally help the world settle disputes *legally*—instead of *lethally*! Discover this workable, practical way you can empower yourself to create prosperity and permanent peace on our planet. 300,000 in print. Released March 1988.

Meeting the Challenge

You can make a difference! Since your future and the life of your family may depend on rapidly replacing the law of force with the force of law, we are making *PlanetHood* available on a nonprofit basis. Please buy as many copies as you can and distribute them quickly.

To help you do this, the list price of *PlanetHood* is $2.50. For only $3 postpaid, we will mail a copy of this book to any person in the world for whom you furnish the name and address. If you buy a case of 100, we will mail the case anywhere in the United States at a cost of $70 postpaid in the U.S. (only 70¢ per book). If you buy 1,000 or more, they will cost only 50¢ per book (a total of $500 including shipping in the U.S.). Send orders to Ken Keyes College Bookroom, 790 Commercial Avenue, Coos Bay, OR 97420. For VISA or MasterCard call (503) 267-4112.

All books available in bookstores or see page 225 for order form.

Two powerful workshops on tape!

Handbook to Higher Consciousness
Ken Keyes, Jr.

$9.95, Cassette,
approximately 1 hour

Includes a
32-page Mini-Guide to
Higher Consciousness

➤ One of the most charismatic and acclaimed philosophers of the New Age, Ken personally brings to you on audiotape his modern, practical blueprint for a life of love and happiness.

➤ Includes a 32-page Mini-Guide to Higher Consciousness that can guide you toward a vibrant, loving, happy, and fulfilled life!

➤ If you've had enough of the up-and-down roller-coastering between pleasure and pain, then you are ready to apply these step-by-step methods to improve your life while you live it!

Gathering Power Through Insight and Love
Ken and Penny Keyes

$15.95, 2 cassettes

Includes a
48-page Workbook

➤ These dynamic cassettes are taken from the popular workshops designed by Ken and Penny Keyes.

➤ Expanding on the principles found in the *Handbook*, Ken and Penny explain and demonstrate specific techniques that can help you put the Living Love Methods to work daily.

➤ Offers practical and precise ways to develop the skills for radically improving the quality of your life.

See pages 224 and 225 for ordering information.

ORDERING INFORMATION

Books

#600	$6.95	Handbook to Higher Consciousness
#670	$5.95	Handbook to Higher Consciousness: The Workbook
#665	$7.95	Discovering the Secrets of Happiness: My Intimate Story
#660	$6.95	Gathering Power Through Insight and Love
#610	$5.95	A Conscious Person's Guide to Relationships
#615	$5.95	Your Life Is a Gift
#605	$5.95	How to Enjoy Your Life in Spite of It All
#620	$4.95	Prescriptions for Happiness
#630	$7.95	Taming Your Mind
#625	$4.95	Your Heart's Desire
#635	$2.00	The Hundredth Monkey
#640	$2.50	PlanetHood

Audio Cassettes

#500	$9.95	Handbook to Higher Consciousness, with a 32-page Mini-Guide
#510	$15.95	Gathering Power Through Insight and Love, two tapes with a 48-page workbook

Music Cassettes (4 for $25.00)

#109	$6.95	Ocean of Love
#110	$6.95	Oneness Space
#115	$6.95	Open Up Your Vision
#120	$6.95	Carry the Love
#125	$6.95	The 12 Pathways in Song

Posters

#315	$3.95	The Twelve Pathways

Other

#800	$9.95	Reprogramming Counter
#645	$6.95	Living Love Songbook (words and music to music cassettes #109, #110, #115, and #120)

For a more complete listing of books, audio and video tapes, posters, and workshops, send for a free catalog to Ken Keyes College, 790 Commercial Avenue, Coos Bay, OR 97420, or telephone (503) 267-6412, Monday through Friday, 9:00 a.m. to 4:30 p.m. Pacific time.

TO ORDER BOOKS AND TAPES

Qty.	Item No.	Item	Price	Amount

Please include shipping and handling charges: $1.50 for the first item, 50¢ for each additional item. **SPECIAL OFFER: If you order 10 items or more you can take off 20%, PLUS we'll pay for shipping and handling.**

Subtotal _____
Shipping _____
TOTAL _____

☐ **Yes!** Please put me on your mailing list and send me a free catalog listing workshops, books, posters, music albums and cassettes, and audio and video tapes.

Ship to: (please print) _____

Address _____

City _____

State _____ Zip _____

Telephone No. ( ) _____

For ( ) VISA or ( ) MasterCard orders only:
Card # _____

Exp. Date _____ Signature: _____

Send order along with your check or money order in U.S. funds to Ken Keyes College Bookroom, Dept. HBWB, 790 Commercial Avenue, Coos Bay, OR 97420. To order by phone with VISA or MasterCard call: (503) 267-4112, Monday through Friday, 9:00 a.m. to 4:30 p.m. Pacific time. Allow up to 4 weeks for delivery via fourth class mail.

RIPOFFS:
Penalties You Pay for Each Addictive Demand

AREA AFFECTED:	YOUR PENALTIES:
1. Body reactions	Tension, clumsiness, weakness, queasiness, constricted breath, pain, sweat, rapid heartbeat, illness.
2. Emotions	Separate-self feelings such as fear, frustration, anger, hate.
3. Attitude toward self	Low self-esteem, limited feeling of love, threat, judgmentalness.
4. Attitude toward other people	Inability to feel close to others, limited or no love, criticalness, judgmentalness.
5. Energy, time	Low energy, time lost, energy wasted in feeling separate about past or future, and in trying to force things.
6. Perception of what is happening in life	Distorted perceptions, inability to appreciate the beauty that is around you, lots of illusions, dulled senses.
7. Spontaneity, creativity, openness	Compulsive behavior, inflexibility, creativity blocked, pushing to make things happen out of fear or anger.
8. Humor	No humor: This is a serious, real, and horrible problem.
9. Cooperative relationships with others	Triggering of others' addictions, unnecessary ego conflicts.
10. Alternatives and choices	Limited perspective, with "tunnel vision" that can only respond automatically and with few options.
11. Making changes	Limited ability and less energy to effect change because of a lack of insight and distorted perception.
12. Enjoying your life	Even if you get what you want, it's never enough: demands escalate. Anxiously protected and defending what you have.

Taken from *Gathering Power Through Insight and Love* by Ken and Penny Keyes, © 1987, Living Love Publications.

PAYOFFS:
Why Your Ego Holds On to an Addictive Demand

I get to be right and make the other person wrong. I get to feel superior. I'll prove it's unfair or untrue.

I get attention, sympathy, agreement, approval, and/or comfort.

I avoid taking responsibility for what I do, say, or feel. I can avoid looking at "what is" in my life. I don't have to really experience what I am feeling.

People will know that I'm (a good teacher, a responsible parent, a caring person, a skilled bricklayer, etc.).

People won't think I'm (egotistical, a coward, etc.).

I have an excuse for poor performance.

I get to avoid confronting the addictions that would come up if I weren't running this addiction.

It feels safe and familiar to hold on to the old pattern and scary to let it go.

I get to play martyr.

I get to play the victim role.

It feels safe to keep a distance from other people (or a specific person).

I get to enjoy the fantasy. ("Even if I don't get what I want, I still get to fantasize about it—food, sex, looking different, etc.")

I get to share and feel close to other people who have the same addictions.

I feel a sense of intensity. ("I feel really alive when I'm angry.")

I'll get control over myself. I won't do it again. I'll be careful about what I do. ("If I demand to not overeat, I won't.")

He/she/they will change. They won't keep doing what they are doing. ("If I get angry enough, they'll agree with me or do what I want.")

They'll make it up to me because they'll see how upset I am and they'll feel sorry or guilty.

Taken from *Gathering Power Through Insight and Love* by Ken and Penny Keyes, © 1987, Living Love Publications.